The T

Charlotte the

Liberator

a novella by

Dewi Heald

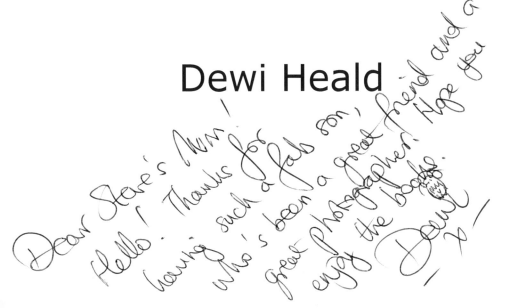

A note on the text :

Charlotte's story was first written in short story format in 2016. It was subsequently expanded to a 30,000 word version for the New Welsh Review novella competition. A 32,500 word version exists, known as the Warr-Britton-Ramage version. This version has been specially formatted for this edition and is 34,446 words long and thus the longest of all the versions. Enjoy!

index

introduction

Every city in the United Kingdom has the same statue. A child in Belfast, Bangor, Nottingham, Norwich, London or Dundee might look up at the woman on that pedestal and ask '*Who is that?*' but their parents will reply with the same information. She is Charlotte the Liberator, the greatest woman that the country has ever produced. She is depicted in every city with her head turned heroically skywards, a tablet computer raised in one hand, a spreadsheet in the other.

The curious thing is that when the 16 year old Charlotte was sitting at the Careers Computer in McDonald's Comprehensive School in Barry, her list of recommended careers did not include 'Revolutionary Leader'.

part one of four :

Charlotte the Teenager

Charlotte threw her bag on to the sofa in the front room and shouted to her mother that she was home. A voice came out of the kitchen asking her how the school day was.

"Okay, s'pose," she said with a yawn.

Charlotte's mother appeared from the kitchen and smiled at her elder daughter.

"I thought it was your booking with the Careers Computer today."

"Yeah, well, you know what it's like. They're not going to say that I can be a doctor or anything."

"True - don't forget your Dad is coming over tonight."

"Yeah sure, Mam."

With that, Charlotte walked off towards the stairs. By the time she had reached them, her mother was shouting after her to pick up her bag but there was no answer. Mumbling testily to herself, Charlotte's mother hung her daughter's bag up for her.

At the top of the stairs, Charlotte saw her sister coming out of the bathroom.

"Hi Heather," she said and thought that she could hear a guitar chord in her head.

"Hey sis, been told at school today what a loser you are - did the computer say 'Future Career - Loser'?"

Charlotte pulled a face at Heather. Two years younger than Charlotte, she could be described as more outgoing, but the description that stuck in Charlotte's mind was the one used by the boys in her year at school, 'She's like a blonde and pretty version of Charlotte'. This did not make for sisterly bonding.

"You'll find it hard to make a career in buffing your nails and sitting on your fat arse," she shot back.

"Oh no, not for me. You forget that I've got this," replied Heather, holding out a handful of her long, blonde hair, carefully straightened earlier, "I'm going to marry a billionaire and he will take me to London and pay for everything!"

Charlotte snorted contemptuously, walked into her room and slammed the door behind her. Behind her, Charlotte's sister was shouting, "Get with the 2040s, sis!"

Charlotte's computer was already on and logged in to EPICchat, so she simply adjusted one of the screens and loaded up a dull, mind-numbing puzzle game on the other.

She typed 'Hi Sadie' into the chat window on EPICchat and immediately a xylophone note was produced. It had been a quirk of the inventor of EPICchat that he thought that whenever anyone greeted anyone else there should be a musical sound. Charlotte now found it hard to meet anyone offline without hearing the sound there too.

Those who saw Charlotte fling her school bag around idly downstairs might have been surprised by the care with which she hung up her jacket on the back of her bedroom door or by the tidiness of her own space. In some ways it was typical of a teenager at the start of the 2040s, one wall filled with the obsessions and interests of childhood, the impossible dreams of horses and exotic places, the other wall covered in teenage obsessions, the impossible dreams of pop stars and films.

Around her computer too there was a sense of organisation. The shelf above it was slightly wonky, but this was a good effort from when she was fourteen and had no parent willing to do it. On the shelf her school GCSE subjects were arranged by folder – Customer Service, Food Technology, Working with the Public, IT, English, Maths and Welsh. Only one folder was not for GCSEs, this was her folder of sports news. Though only a moderate hockey player whose games teacher had once remarked on her skill 'when hitting other people with a stick', Charlotte loved everything to do with sport and if the stars of Cardiff City FC were not on posters on her wall, it was only because she believed that theirs was a profession too serious for teenage fandom.

The screen showing EPICchat flashed a new message.

S> Hi Princess

'Princess' was Charlotte's nickname, coming from the joke that she shared her name with a royal princess. She could almost hear the royal fanfare that sounded on Sadie's computer when the phrase was entered.

C> Hiya. Dull day. You?

The puzzle game on the other screen involved matching rows of coloured fruit and Charlotte idly matched up strawberries and cherries, as she did most nights.

S> Okay. Did you speak to the Careers Computer? What did it say?

C> Doctor. Lawyer. Civil Engineer

S> Wow!

C> Course not. Usual thing. Need more customer service skills to make it to call centre

S> Stop dodging language lessons then, Princess?

C> Huh. Bet Princess Charlotte Windsor didn't have a Careers Computer session – can you imagine – "What skills do you have? What jobs are open to you - oh yeah, Princess."

S> Way it is. We all do what we're born to do. Even she has a life set out for her

Charlotte shook her head and went back to matching pairs of pears. Something about this careers thing did not sit well with her. What if she did want to be a doctor?

S> Jim in Biology wants to know chances of date with your sister?

C> fd;lobghdfojgnfdlkgnfdlkn

S> You kay?

C> Sorry, too angry to type. Just had an earful from the sis, says she's marrying a rich man as her career plan

S> Oh, studied that in Feminism. It's called Allsop Theory after a woman who told girls to forget about education and get married. It's quite central to feminist theory, women can do this but men can't, it's our advantage

C> Don't like this feminism thing, all about being nice to men. Shouldn't we try to be equal?

S> LOL. You say craziest things

There was a pause again while Charlotte went back to her game. To be honest, a frustrating day at McDonald's Comprehensive School was not being helped by Sadie, best friend status or not.

S>Have you got the PDF for tomorrow's biology lesson?

C> You in e-learning again? I've got it on memory stick, I'll pass it over

Charlotte paused her game and switched off the chat window too. Sadie would know how organised Charlotte was and, sure enough, she reached up to a plastic box on the end of the shelf containing memory sticks. They had been issued at the start of the year with all the information that students needed, so that they could study on their own if necessary. She picked out one with an orange sticker on it. She had decided that orange was biology.

Charlotte walked over to the window of her bedroom and opened it. She placed the memory stick in a small brown basket and then reached for a 'grabbing hand' toy that had been bought years ago to enable this operation. The plastic grabbing hand gripped around the basket handle and Charlotte held it out of the window. Six feet away, Sadie was using the same toy from her own bedroom window and Charlotte felt a tug on the basket and a shout of 'target acquired'. That was her signal to release the grabbing hand and pull it back to her bedroom. This was a system of exchange which had worked almost perfectly for years, the unfortunate incident of the make-up that fell on the dachshund from number forty-three being the only glitch in the operation.

S> Ta

C> Can't chat for long - Dad's coming over

S> Sure

Charlotte thought that she heard a sound from downstairs - that would be Dad.

C> Gotta go. He's here

A squeal from Heather rang out up the stairs as Charlotte walked down.

"Who's my little princess?" her Dad was asking as he nuzzled Heather to his side. Charlotte wondered what the sister was after – new shoes, a night out, approval for dating Jim from biology class? "And Charlotte, good to see you too."

"Hi Dad," said Charlotte but there was no sound in her head to accompany this greeting. Dad was old and therefore the rules of EPICchat did not apply to him.

Charlotte smiled with the kind of 'I'm not really interested in this' cool that teenagers bring to everything that they really care about. He held out a hand to shake hers but this studied formality worked under her skin and she gave him a big hug, displacing Heather. Her father felt warm and smelt of old jumpers, the night air and re-assurance. He just laughed and smiled.

"Are you helping your Mam?" he asked and the two girls looked away guiltily.

Charlotte's Dad sighed and made his way to the front room.

"Steve," was the formal greeting from Charlotte's Mam, annoying both her daughters, who disliked hearing their parents called by names other than their proper names, 'Mam' and 'Dad'.

"Do you need any help, Maria?"

Charlotte's Mam nodded and her ex-husband turned to his daughters and motioned towards the kitchen. Both did a mixture of rolling eyes, sighing and muttering 'Oh, Dad!' before heading into the kitchen to set out the table, make drinks and do all the tasks that they knew needed doing but had to be told to do each time.

"You're looking good, Maria."

"No, I'm not," replied Charlotte's Mam and she was right, she looked older than her years, tired and ill.

"I can help you with the hospital bills, you know that," Charlotte's Dad whispered in a low voice so that his daughters would not hear.

"You've got Tameka to think of now as well, you don't want to be worrying about me," came the muttered reply.

At this moment Charlotte's Dad stepped forward to embrace her Mam, but she only allowed it for a brief few seconds. He stepped back and looked at her.

"I don't want the girls growing up without you. If you need money for the pills or for the hospital visits, you just ask."

"The girls are doing quite all right without me, I think and ..." but then Charlotte's Mam stopped in mid-sentence to acknowledge the generosity of the offer, "thank you, I will probably have to take you up on that."

It was not often that Charlotte's family sat down to dinner and the pile of used plates in Heather's room would have been witness to this. Charlotte did at least manage to take her plates from her bedroom to a pile next to the dishwasher. Her mother was working on teaching her the skills of loading them into the dishwasher. One of the exceptions to this rule was Meat Night, when they would all meet together, Dad included, to share a meal involving meat.

"Tonight it's jacket potatoes, with a tuna mayo mix – it's mayo and dairy-free mayola because I was running out of both – and then salad, some cherry tomatoes and a few other bits," announced Charlotte's Mam as she ferried bowls to the table.

Heather was looking into a bowl of salad suspiciously, "Where's the meat?" she asked.

"There's no meat this week," said Charlotte's Mam, "I didn't get enough hours on my contract this week to afford any. We'll be on fish this week."

The children looked at her with disappointment but could see their father's face cautioning them against comment.

"Thank you, Maria," he said and his children nodded grudging approval.

Helping herself to the largest potato, Heather announced, "Of course, when I am married to a rich man, he will bring me meat every day."

"You'd better to learn to cook then," muttered Charlotte.

"No, sis," countered Heather, "we will have servants for that. I will inspect the latest meat from our country estate and then pass it to the servants to cook for me. I will ... I will do whatever rich wives do."

Charlotte grabbed the bowl of potatoes from her sister while their parents laughed. The number of country estates in Barry was not large. The number of rich men in Barry was not large. There were probably servants, but more opportunities to be one than to have one.

"How did the Careers Computer go today, Charly?" asked Dad.

"Alright, I s'pose," replied Charlotte, arranging her salad around her potato.

"Said she was going to remain a loser," added her sister, predictably.

"Now now, we all have different talents ..." started their father.

"Yours isn't knowing when to keep your big mouth shut," fired Charlotte towards her sister.

"You'll be first up against the wall when the revolution comes!" declared Heather.

"What does that even mean? People say that all the time but what wall? What ...?"

"It means that when I've married my rich husband, we'll buy one of those private police forces and lock the likes of you up for being dull."

"What if he doesn't want to do everything you say?"

"He'll be old and in poor health. He'll be swept away by my beauty, but he will also have a dodgy heart which means ..."

Heather's voice trailed off as she saw her father's face turn from light-hearted indulgence to eyes wide annoyance.

"Oh God, sorry Mam. Mam, I didn't mean ..."

There was an awkward silence as the father and his daughters looked at their ex-wife and mother respectively to see if she had been offended.

"Girls," their Mam muttered, in this temporary cessation in hostilities, "Will you just eat your potatoes in peace for once? Charlotte – at least your sister has a plan ..."

Heather gave her sister a smug smile that gloated all the way across the table and back.

"... it's a stupid plan, I grant you ..."

"Mam!" yelled Heather and it was Charlotte's turn to gloat.

"...but it is a plan nonetheless. You're sixteen now, education ends, you need to think about your own plan. Your sister has another two years of school."

There was silence as the family ate their food and the sisters exchanged bitter looks. Their parents made light and meaningless remarks about the weather, the weeds in the backyard and the possibility of the road being resurfaced along Aberystwyth Crescent. It was only after a while that Charlotte's Dad said the first thing that Charlotte had found useful all meal –

"I've got a memory stick with Liverpool versus Chelsea on it, fancy watching it after you've cleared up?"

Charlotte smiled. She had no idea where she would be next September, but she knew that there would be sport on television. It was a rare certainty for her.

*   *   *   *   *

Charlotte and her father stretched out on the long, leather sofa and studied the team formations on the screen across the room.

"Chelsea are packing midfield by the look of it," observed Charlotte, her head nodding back and forth as she thought about the names and the structure in front of her.

"That's because Liverpool have got Evans up front again. He's one hell of a lad – you know he's from up the road in Llanharan."

"Everyone knows that, Dad. That's the thing, isn't it? Why is it in football you can grow up to be a millionaire but in nothing else? And why is it only male footballers? Why is no-one paying Shania Wilson or Louise McGougan to go to Dubai and play in this kind of game?"

"How did we manage to raise you and your sister in the same household?" asked Charlotte's father with a chuckle, aiming to ignore his daughter's questions as awkwardly as if they had been about where babies came from.

Charlotte noted that Evans was indeed up front for Liverpool. The Manager had thrown Speedman in to the centre as playmaker and Charlotte wondered if he was really at peak fitness after a recent run of games in different countries across the world. She decided to answer her father's question instead.

"I listened to you when you lived here, Dad, that's how. You and your mates chatting away about penalties and goal difference and offside and zonal marking systems. I was always interested in how you organise a team. The little princess up there was always more interested in glitter and dolls and anything pink."

15

"You mustn't be rude about your sister now, Charly."

"It's why our school hockey team won everything for three years. I was unofficially coaching them on positional play – moving in triangular formations, everything I learnt from you."

Charlotte's Dad reached over and ruffled her hair with his right hand. It was a strange way to express his pride, but it would do. He also knew that his other daughter would have screamed if anyone had touched her hair. They settled down to their match, he with a beer, she with water, swapping opinions on the formations, the play and that frankly off-side penalty that should never have been given three minutes into extra time.

"Dad?" asked Charlotte, as her father looked for the remote control so he could fast forward through the adverts, "Is she going to die?"

"How many times do I need to tell you, you must not kill your sister."

"Dad! You know what I mean."

Charlotte's father spoke in a hushed tone, even though her mother was not within earshot.

"I don't know. She just has to keep taking the pills, visiting the hospital and hopefully her heart will hold out. You do know that the problem is ..."

"Dad, it's hereditary. Don't you think I've read every damn book and online article about it?"

"Sorry, I ..." started the man but there were no words to complete his sentence.

"I just don't get it. I might also have a heart problem, that's hereditary. But is it hereditary to be poor, live in

Barry, do the same job as everyone else and struggle to pay the bills?"

"Everything costs money, darling. Your school costs money, your Mam's medicine costs money, everything costs money. It's the way it is. It would be silly to fight it. Money is the root of all happiness, they say."

Charlotte was not satisfied with the answer, but she knew that it was the best one that she was going to receive. She moved over the sofa and put her arms around her father. He was not a big man, but her arms only just stretched all the way around him. He chortled slightly, astonished but happy at his daughter's actions. He felt her fear of losing her mother and knew that there was nothing he could say to truly re-assure her.

"Look," he said instead, "they're bringing Argyle on for the second half!"

"His average pass completion rate in recent games isn't going to help," noted Charlotte, knowing that this was about the only re-assurance that she was going to receive.

* * * * *

"Heather Jo! Get your arse down here immediately!"

This was the sound of Charlotte's mother shouting up the stairs as time ticked on before school. Charlotte sat at the table in the kitchen munching on some cereal sleepily.

"Where is that girl?" her mother repeated.

It was another five minutes before Heather breezed in, blonde hair flowing behind her as she explained that she could not possibly stop for breakfast.

"I was going to do you eggs on toast."

"I'll just take the toast then, ta," said Heather, grabbing a piece from the toaster and munching on it. The crumbs formed a little trail across the kitchen. "I don't like eating breakfast, it's not good for you."

"You spend too long doing your make-up, that's the trouble," muttered Charlotte.

"Can I help being the beautiful one in the family?"

"Stop here one minute, young lady!"

Heather turned around and stood sulkily while her mother hoisted her tie to its proper height, did up all her shirt buttons and then rolled her skirt down so that it was at least within shouting distance of her knees.

"That's a little better. You know breakfast is the most important meal of the day."

"Sure Mam, can't delay or I'll miss the gang. Bye-ee!"

With no time for more protest, Hurricane Heather blew out of the kitchen towards the door.

"Is it really so long ago," asked Charlotte's mother, partly to her daughter and partly to no-one, "that you girls would give me a big kiss on the cheek, tell me that you loved me and then go off to school together?"

"Whatever, Mam," said Charlotte, leaving her cereal bowl out on the table, "Sadie'll be here any minute, gotta fly!"

Sure enough there was soon a knock at the door and Charlotte was gone within the minute too.

"Hi Sadie," [ping!]

"Hi Princess," [royal fanfare!]

The two girls walked to school together almost every day. It was not far from Aberystwyth Crescent, but there was enough time to catch up on any gossip that had occurred before they last spoke (the night before).

"You've got e-learning Biology first," said Charlotte.

"Yeah, sure – you're language lab, aren't you?" replied her friend.

"Yes, more customer service training. How many times do I need to tell people that I don't care about their broken toaster?"

Sadie nodded, "We need to know stuff like this though for doing jobs. I thought someone like you would have had a plan for next year."

Charlotte shook her head in a manner that said 'don't ask'. They walked down towards the waterfront in silence. The school was further along the main road towards the old Victorian docks building.

"Oh, oh, oh! Goss, goss, goss!" said Sadie suddenly with excitement, as they waited at the traffic lights, "You know Jim from my Biology class?"

"You told me last night that he wanted a date with my parents' failure to replicate their early creation of perfection?"

"Well, Sara-Louise messaged me last night. He's been suspended. Apparently, he cornered one of the Food Technology girls in the Learning Resource Centre and ... ugh, you know ... kind of pushed himself up against her onto a bookshelf."

"That's awful! Is she all right?"

"She grabbed a copy of the Complete Works of Jane Austen and hit him in the groin."

"Including the unpublished works?"

"And letters to her sister!"

"That must have hurt."

"I hope so!"

"Thank goodness she appreciates good literature," said Charlotte.

Jim was a sleazeball then, no surprises there.

"Why do we do it? Why do we always spend the walk to school gossiping about boys?" asked Charlotte.

Sadie looked puzzled and answered back quickly, "Because we're girls – jeez Princess, did you not notice puberty?"

"I mean, why not school or family or what we want to do next year, I don't know ..."

The two friends walked past a huge billboard showing a picture of a happy-looking woman and the slogan, "Oh, I couldn't go without my coffee in the morning!"

"You make me laugh, Princess, honestly you do. You need to stop thinking about it all. Maybe it's because love is the only thing we control. School's got a timetable, we know the kind of job that we'll have, love's the only unpredictable thing."

"And football. And hockey. Mam doesn't like me watching women's rugby, of course."

"I keep telling you, you know what they say, it's not cool for girls to sweat."

"Well, if I am supposed to be attracting slimeballs like Jim, then I think that I will choose sweat."

"You do make me LOL, Princess, you really do."

They walked on together in silence, taking a few moments to cross the final busy road down to the school.

"How was your Dad?" asked Sadie as the school gates were in sight, "Are they still married, your two?"

"Yeah, Mam says it's too expensive and difficult to get a divorce, so they haven't bothered."

"Makes sense. Thought your Dad had a new girlfriend though?"

"Yeah, Tameka. It's okay though, she's married to someone else still too."

"That's fair enough then. Never did understand why they made divorce so expensive."

"To keep people together is the usual explanation."

"That works then," said Sadie approvingly.

* * * * *

It was a chance meeting at the school Careers Fayre that day which was to take Charlotte's life in a new direction and a step onwards on the path to glory. There was no stall at the fayre for the recruitment of revolutionary leaders, but why would there be? The history books explained that there had never been any kind of revolution or uprising in Britain and that it stood proudly as a country governed by wise and generous men since its foundation. All the same, it might have been fun to have found Che Guevara and Martin Luther King sitting behind a table in a comprehensive school in Barry trying to sell to schoolchildren their very different views of taking on power.

For the most part, the stalls were linked to different branches and different types of fast food outlets. Charlotte saw Sadie queuing up to talk to a recruitment consultant for the pizza takeaway on the road to Barry Docks.

"Hi Princess," – royal fanfare – "Language lab okay?"

"Hi Sadie," – ping! – "how many times can you practise 'How may I direct your call? Biology okay?"

"Yeah, thanks for the memory stick. We just followed the computer and it was fine. Your notes were great. Where did you go for lunch?"

"Sat down by the football field for a change."

"You analysing the football team's tactics again? You know that they complained about you criticising them."

"They should be so lucky. They're never worth watching anyway. Everyone wants to be a striker. They don't understand that in a team you only win when everyone works together in their own role for the good of the whole."

"Not checking out Steve with the long hair?"

"He's one of the worst for not passing when there's a shooting opportunity."

"He's also gay ... so Andrea says, at least."

"Oh."

"Ha! I know what you were doing – isn't that where your sister and her crowd hang out, down by the trees at the bottom of the field? You're checking up on her!"

"I am not! My ability to care about the sister is comfortably at zero."

"You're a weird girl, Charlotte. Hold on, my turn."

The queue moved forwards and Sadie went to talk to a man who could explain how a career in the pizza delivery business could be stable and satisfying with excellent opportunities to stay in the same job.

Charlotte wandered on and was immediately struck by the sight of a man sitting on his own at the end of the tables. He was wearing a flat cap indoors, which struck her as unusual, and he had glasses and a kindly smile. No-one seemed to be talking to him, so she decided to go and sit in front of him to make his day worthwhile.

"Hi, I'm Charlotte, tell me what it is like to work in ... err ...," she looked at a desk calendar in front of the man, "Niton Reprographics."

"They printed the calendar."

"Okay, what it is like to work in ..."

Charlotte's eyes darted around the table for a few moments before she thought to look at his badge. His name was Dean and he worked for 'Abacus – you can count on us!'

"I've always wanted to work for Abacus," she said.

Dean the Abacus Man took off his flat cap to expose a small amount of grey hair and a large amount of bald patch.

"Why would that be?" he asked, sounding less than convinced.

"Because we're the people you can count on!"

Dean rubbed his eyes and smiled. The girl could read and was vaguely intelligent, she would pass the entry test without problems.

"You've never heard of Abacus, have you?"

"I would like you to tell me more about it," countered Charlotte, deciding that she would give nothing away.

"Well," said Dean, impressed by her ability to dodge a question, "do you remember those playing fields up the hill by Port Road?"

"Yes, of course, my hockey team used to practise there."

"Well, they've been sold to us and we're building a new office there."

"So there'll be no more hockey?"

"No, but think of it this way. What benefits the economy of Barry more – a playing field or an office block? How many people does a playing field employ after all?"

Charlotte was a little taken aback about the loss of that playing field. Sure, she had not been there for a little while and she had heard rumours that on a Sunday morning it was littered with used cigarettes, used cans of cheap cider and used condoms, but at least the field was used.

Dean, meanwhile, was feeling that he was losing a potentially good recruit and having spent much of the afternoon being ignored (even resorting to wearing his flat cap indoors to try to attract attention), he changed tack.

"We've been selling and managing insurance in the USA for over a hundred years. Our UK branch was founded by an American man named 'Barry' and some years ago he discovered that there was a place called Barry in South Wales, so he wanted an office here. It's quite a funny story really, when you think about it."

Charlotte thought about it. Dean was pausing to see if Charlotte laughed. She did not laugh.

"We have lots of exciting opportunities in telesales, customer complaints and telemarketing – how are your language skills?"

Charlotte adopted an overly-cheery voice, "Your call is being held in a queue. It is important to us, a customer operative will be with you shortly."

Dean laughed but wagged a finger at her, "Now we replaced those people with computers a long, long time ago!"

Charlotte picked up one of his leaflets and scanned the picture of the office building on the site of one of her team's most impressive goals.

Dean was continuing, "We have a great working environment, a decent pay band and there are many young people like yourself starting in the next intake so you would have a chance to meet other young people, hang out with ... err ... boys."

Charlotte raised her eyebrows at him and it only made him feel more awkward about being a middle-aged man using the word 'boys'.

"You have to pass an entry test of course, but you would have no trouble, I am sure. Is there any particular area of insurance that interests you?"

"I don't know," said Charlotte honestly and started to arrange the flyers on his desk into neat piles.

"I'll have a look on the school system," said Dean, producing a hand-sized computer from under the desk and tapping some keys on it.

He read Charlotte's school report notes. She turned up to lessons, she made a contribution and she loved sport. There in the middle of these notes was something unusual though. This girl before him was clearly very good at organising things. His neat stacks of flyers could have told him that but the school computer system noted it repeatedly.

Dean looked up at Charlotte and smiled.

"Have you ever heard of administration?" he asked.

part two of four :

Charlotte the Administrator

"Hi, I'm Barry," announced a brash American from the large TV screen in the conference room of Abacus Insurance.

Charlotte sat among a room full of new recruits, all nervously fiddling with their information packs and clipboards. It had been weird seeing the sister head downhill to school in the morning while she walked uphill to the Abacus offices. This was working life then, what she had spent eleven years in school being prepared for. To be honest, her initial impression was that it was much like school, the important thing was to smile and pretend that you were enjoying yourself.

She had been given an orange badge when she arrived (orange means biology, she remembered from long ago), but she found herself in a sea of blue, green and red badges.

Barry was still talking. He had founded Abacus Insurance many years ago as a car insurance company but the expansion in the UK had been built on health insurance. What better place to expand than in little old 'Barry, England' he was saying with a chuckle. Luckily, there were still plenty of ill people to keep the business going. He sounded as though he viewed ill-health as good for business and Charlotte looked around at the other school leavers and wondered if they knew anyone who was ill.

The lights came up in the conference room and a man named Terry ('I'm Terry, but you can call me Terry' had been his pre-film opening line) with grey hair and a pink tie thrown back over his shoulder took centre stage.

"Barry, our founder, who sadly died last year," he announced.

Charlotte found it hard not to laugh about a man enthusiastic about ill-health dying young. No-one else was laughing.

"He never got to see his vision of an office in Barry come to pass. He was a visionary, a man of genius. Why 'Abacus'? It is an unwritten rule of the insurance industry that people only buy insurance from companies whose names begin with an A, B, C or D. Admiral, Diamond, Direct Line, Churchill ... you name it, they are all alphabet starters. That is why Abacus was brilliant. He had his stroke of genius all those years ago and then, of course, sadly last year he had his stroke ... and ... err ... I never met the great man, of course, but ..."

Was Terry becoming a little misty-eyed?

"... he was a man who can inspire us to be the greatest that we can be."

Charlotte found a pen in her induction pack and started doodling.

Terry gave a short overview of holidays (very few), sickness (you are not allowed to be sick) and pregnancy (employees should avoid becoming pregnant, especially the male ones ... ha ha) and then they were divided by badge colour. A small, serious-looking, middle-aged woman named Barbara shook Charlotte's hand and led her – the only orange badge – away to another room.

The Administration Department had a small office at the back of a long and wide 'hotdesking' room. Charlotte had the impression from Barbara that they were generally seen as a different species and largely avoided. There were four chairs in the admin room and eight computers. This prompted Charlotte's first question.

"Why does everyone have two computers?"

Barbara gave a nervous and slightly apologetic grin that said that she knew that what she was about to say could be nonsense but what can you do?

"Abacus is actually two companies – Count On Us Insurance and ABC Holdings. They merged a few years ago and they had different computer systems. We had to just get up and running together, so there are two systems. It's easier if we have two computers each, one for each system."

"Why don't you just put all the information on one system?"

Barbara laughed and shook her head, "That would take so much time."

There was no-one else in the office at that moment but Charlotte was told that she would have two other colleagues in there, Tina and Tom. There were strict delineations about who did payroll, who looked after filing systems and who had a key to the filing cabinet. In the first six months, Charlotte was not expected to use the filing cabinet. She walked up to the slightly-damaged metal thing and gave it a pat as if to say 'one day, I will' but as her hand passed close to it, a spark of static electricity hit her.

"Ow! You've got it booby-trapped?"

"Ha, no, just be careful on the carpet, it will give you a static build-up."

"Will my hair stand on end?"

"Only when it's timesheet time each month."

Timesheets were to be Charlotte's domain. Each month she had to collect them from Abacus's hundred staff, add the hours to a master timesheet and then confirm them for the purposes of payroll. It sounded an easy, if dull, task until she realised the first problem of any administration in Abacus.

"These are the Count On Us timesheets and these are the ABC timesheets."

"No!"

"Yes, we haven't really merged them yet."

"And they're all on paper?"

"So that they can be signed off, yes. You add them to the master timesheet file on the computer- that's this one here."

"'Timesheets - FINAL?"

"Yes ... err ... no, actually, I think it's now 'Timesheets - FINAL FINAL' below."

"What about that one - 'Timesheets - FINAL FINAL 2'?"

"Ah yes, that must be it."

"Why don't you save things with the date on the end? For instance, 'Timesheets FINAL 251046 if you save it that day but then 'Timesheets FINAL 261046' if you save a new copy the next day."

Barbara smiled weakly and placed a re-assuring arm on Charlotte.

"That would just get confusing. Now, when you are done, print out the timesheets and file them by month in the bottom drawer of the filing cabinet – Tom can lend you his key when you need it."

Charlotte stared at Barbara and wondered what she had let herself in for.

"Any questions?" asked Barbara, as if she had explained everything perfectly.

"No," replied Charlotte dutifully, though she had so, so many questions.

The first six months in your first job always involve the sheer joy of realising that someone will pay you money. No-one should underrate the happiness that is brought by the idea that at the end of every month, money will appear in your bank account.

Initially, Charlotte had intended to keep a low-profile and try not to be sacked, but she could not take in the timesheets each month without a feeling of annoyance. This – the system and the annoyance – had to change.

Firstly, Charlotte designed a new timesheet that could be used by both sides of the company. Count On Us were known as the less reliable ones, so she worked with them first to explain it. It would also be electronic, so it could be submitted at the click of a button and signed off at the click of a button each month. She would still print them and store them, but by payroll number instead of name, in the ... ow!

Tom smiled at her every time this happened. He was a kindly man with a straggly beard and a pleasant smile. Although he had no intention of working as hard as

Charlotte did, he had sympathy for a woman regularly electrocuted by a filing cabinet.

"I've tried so many different bloody shoes!" she yelled at the cabinet one day.

"Have my key," Tom said with a sigh.

"Thank you, but I ... what, you mean, have your key?"

"Yes. I don't do much filing to be honest, you've barely been here six months and you know where everything is. Take it. I can always borrow it if I need one."

That was the last day that the filing cabinet electrocuted Charlotte.

Within a year, Charlotte had decided that all the systems needed to be online. A complicated system still existed for expenses, involving multiple receipts and sign-offs and she wanted to integrate this in with an overall HR package to manage everything that a staff member could need.

Barbara was cautious but also keen to take any credit should Charlotte's idea work. She managed to arrange for Charlotte to make a pitch to pink tie Terry several months later. Being electrocuted by a fling cabinet was going to be nothing compared to the pain of explaining innovation to him.

Charlotte worked for weeks on her presentation. Her mother complained that they no longer saw her in the evenings, the sister barely noticed her disappearance, but she knew that this was a rare chance to improve things for everyone.

When the day finally came and she strode into the meeting room with a clutch of handouts and Barbara following nervously in her wake, she was confident, she was clear and she knew what she was doing. It made sense to her.

Terry Pinktie (as she now called him) stared at the graphs, looking as though he was ready to be called out to something more important at any minute. He was really only there to stop Barbara nagging him.

"You want a computer system?" he said at the end of Charlotte's presentation.

"Yes."

"I'm sorry, Miss ... Charlotte, but we already have two computer systems, a third is just going to cause chaos."

"No, I don't mean a third system, I mean one system."

"We all want one system, but you know that the ABC people think that it is not that easy. They can't just all move on to the other system"

Charlotte could sense which side of the company Terry came from.

"We satisfy both sides by having them both transfer to a whole new system."

Terry sat back in his seat and shook his head at her naïvety.

"You're only a young girl, you'll learn, but things cost money. We can't just invent something new – think of the time spent training people, the disruption to business ... the waste of my time."

"It was only a vague idea that Charlotte came up with on her own," added Barbara quickly.

"On the contrary," said Charlotte with the confidence of someone who had never liked being told what to do and was not going to start liking it now, "I have done this cost-benefit analysis. It envisages a hardware swap on a Sunday – statistically our least busy day –

and then training on a Monday. A whole company approach actually causes less disruption than a team by team approach. The HR admin systems go on there and we give staff control of their own HR records, meaning less admin time at our end. You save money – here's a Gantt Chart showing the stages of development of the project."

Terry looked at the A3 chart in front of him and saw rows of coloured blobs marked against dates. There were more red blobs than green blobs. He had no idea what it all meant, but it was colourful.

"There are a lot more red blobs than green blobs," he said, as if it were a deep insight into the chart in front of him.

"I see that you have immediately seen the risk," replied Charlotte, guessing that flattery was important at this stage and smiling to herself as she saw Barbara nod and repeat 'risk' as she spoke, "but if you look at the costs over the next year, then overall the financial saving is on the projections graph on the other side."

Terry turned over the chart and then whistled through his teeth when he saw the number indicating the potential financial saving. He had already thought that if HR functions were going to be done by employees, they could probably afford to lose an admin worker. Not Charlotte, as thankfully the law allowed them to pay under 21s less than anyone else, so she was valuable.

"These are impressive numbers," he said.

"I thought that when I was helping Charlotte develop this project," added Barbara, with no trace of shame.

"The more I think about it, the more I see that as backing up my plans for consolidation in the next year

..." pondered Terry out loud, then directly to Charlotte, "can you make these numbers work?"

"The whole business is completely inefficient every day we use several systems."

"Perhaps a scoping exercise ..." muttered Terry.

"I could write you a summary of the project plan for you to present to your next Board meeting," offered Charlotte.

Terry drew a hand over his face and then snapped his pink tie from back over his shoulder to hanging downwards again. It was as if this downward motion gave him the energy to spring to his feet.

"Get it done, Charlotte. Good work Barbara too. Excellent."

With that, he gathered up the papers and left the meeting room. Charlotte smiled as she knew that when people start taking credit for your work, it means that they like it.

Charlotte's advocacy of one computer system – delivered six months late but crucially delivered under budget – made her name at Abacus. Increasingly she was seen as the person to go to for ideas on improving systems or introducing new spreadsheets. She was still the most junior administrator, but this hardly mattered to her. The price of her co-operation with Terry's fiction that he had written the business plan for the new computer system was the establishment of a staff hockey team. This met for around six months, until the lack of places to play meant that Charlotte had to finally abandon it. She did, however, become an informal coach to a football team made up of men who worked on the second floor.

Her eighteenth birthday passed without much ceremony beyond a meal out with Mam, Dad and the sister. Heather was less grumpy now that she was approaching the end of school too and had her sights set on a job in the Kwik-Foods supermarket chain. Charlotte wondered how someone so surly could pass customer service modules, but the sister seemed to do it. Dad and Tameka had broken up so she even got to spend more time with him watching football highlights.

She dated from time to time. Mostly it was men from the office – even Tom before he was sacked in a restructuring caused by the streamlining of office admin systems – and a couple of the guys from the second floor football team. That was until they became insecure about her knowing more about football than they did.

Generally Charlotte relaxed into a life of administration, her own little corner of the office surrounded by colour-coded folders and well-ordered files, a couple of stress balls under the desk the only sign that she was ever anything but in control of operations. She was happy with her life and she measured the turning of the earth not in the passing of the seasons but in the quarterly reports for each financial year.

Her fifth anniversary in the job passed barely noticed by anyone else. Charlotte had settled down into the life of quiet frustration which was the lot of most employees. She was thankful to have a job and never imagined that just ahead was a huge change that would take her another big step on the path towards her destiny.

* * * * *

It was shortly after Charlotte's 21st birthday that destiny came and knocked loudly on her door. She had no ambition beyond the insurance office at this point. It was, after all, the kind of job that people from Barry did. Sadie had settled in to the pizza delivery business, the sister was in the supermarket, everywhere the world seemed to have found round holes for all these round pegs to fit in. Charlotte was a square peg, but a square peg will fit in a round hole if its edges are worn down enough.

She arrived at work one morning and felt an excited buzz in the office. She had assumed that this was due to a consignment of cake left by an overly enthusiastic manager who had hit his sales targets, but enquiries with the rest of the team said otherwise. Someone from London was coming to visit.

Charlotte's knowledge of London was about as comprehensive as a Londoner's knowledge of Wales and so she listened with some interest to the talk about Ladislau the Documentary Producer from Heron Productions who would be calling in. She knew the name from a documentary about homophobia in British sport but she tended to ignore the rest of Channel 6's output as they were mostly documentaries with titles like, 'The Boy With Fourteen Feet' or 'The Man Who Thought He Was A Penguin : Revisited'.

Ladislau was coming to Barry to make a documentary about how poor people live and he had wanted to shoot sequences in the insurance offices to show how a public park had been put to much better use for the benefit of all. Being an outsider made him exotic to most people and hence the buzz.

Certainly when he arrived at the office, he had the look of a man who enjoyed sharp suits and expensive moisturiser. His smile was fixed and he shook hands with a large number of people as he said, "Ladislau, Heron Productions, good to meet you" over and over again. Charlotte preferred to stay at her desk, colour-coding a spreadsheet.

Indeed, Charlotte did not meet the mysterious Londoner until the end of the day. Ladislau had asked about the expenses system so that he could charge the business for his travel from London. Management may have known very little about Charlotte, but they did know that she had designed the company expenses system and so sent him to the admin office.

Ladislau entered the admin area to find Charlotte on her own, sitting at one end bouncing a stress toy shaped like a rugby ball off the back wall.

"Ladislau, Heron Productions," he announced, bounding forwards with the same energy that he reserved especially for everyone.

"I know who you are," replied Charlotte without looking at him.

Ladislau was a little shocked by this and withdrew his arm. Everyone loved him and was thrilled to meet a man from London, especially women.

"Rugby fan, are you?" he asked, looking at the shape of the toy bouncing off the wall and back into Charlotte's hands.

"Not really – used to like hockey, but what happened ... oh yes, someone built an office block where the team used to practice."

Ladislau's smile weakened somewhat. He was not used to being challenged.

"I'm looking for Charlotte the Administrator," he tried in the hope that this was her stroppy assistant.

"I am she!" declared Charlotte, turning around to face him for the first time.

He had to admit that she was an attractive woman. She could do with decent make-up and clothes, but having always made his judgements based on what might be seen on a camera, he warmed to her despite her failure to find him fascinating.

"Your sports coverage really lacks depth," she continued with a smile.

"I beg your pardon? Our football highlights are one of our top packages! You know nothing about sport or television, clearly."

Charlotte placed the rugby ball toy into a mug on her desk. What had started as an idle dislike was turning into a determined annoyance.

"The highlights are too short and you never give the viewer a sense of how much of the match has been played. Okay, sure Liverpool are one up, but how much time is left for Arsenal to equalise? You don't press the guests either – it's a bunch of blokes chatting about how great they are. You need to get more into the tactics of the game, talk about formations, width, sitting back and going forwards ..."

Ladislau was now moving to a point of very surprised about this young woman. He sat down on a spare office chair and debated the point.

"What do you mean by 'a bunch of blokes chatting'? I hope that you're not calling me sexist. There is nothing sexist about Channel 6. Half of all our presenters are female, so we can't be said to discriminate."

"Stacey on the sports highlights? She's never been near a sports field in her life."

"She goes to the gym three times a week, I assure you."

Charlotte huffed contemptuously. It was only then that she realised that she was alone in a windowless area with a man who appeared to fancy her, though probably not as much as he fancied himself. She guessed that he never fancied any woman as much as he fancied himself, he was clearly his first and greatest love.

"I've got a copy of the Complete Works of Jane Austen," she said with a sudden nervousness, "so no funny business!"

Ladislau of Heron Productions adjusted his tie and then his cufflinks. He smiled a smile that had a little more re-assurance in it now. Reaching into his jacket pocket, he pulled out a small camera.

"Perhaps you'd like to show Stacey how it should be done?"

Charlotte sighed. Why not? She fixed her mouth into an over-enthusiastic smile and looked straight into the camera.

"Coming up after the break we've got coverage of Liverpool's big match against Middlesbrough. Will Liverpool be playing Williams up front or are they going to take the more defensive option at the Riverside? Middlesbrough have been strong at home this season, we'll be showing you what happens after the break. Also, later we chat to West Ham's new Manager about whether staying in the top league is still an option. See you in three!"

Ladislau sounded genuinely surprised as he said, "That's good, that's good! Shame that Liverpool don't have a player named Williams and they aren't playing Middlesbrough this week."

"Liverpool Women's Team do and they have a crunch FA Cup match against Middlesbrough tonight, but you won't be showing it."

Ladislau switched the camera off and put it back in his pocket.

"Look, I only came here to ask about my expenses claim," he said, "but if you want to write me a critique of everything that is wrong with our highlights show then I will gladly consider it."

At that point, Barbara returned from her lunch break. Silence fell and Charlotte printed out an expenses claim form for Ladislau.

"Bring me a copy of your tickets and sign here, here and here," she said.

"Of course. It was a pleasure to meet you Charlotte the Administrator."

"Bring me back the form and I will sort your expenses out."

It would be hard to think of a situation where two people could leave a conversation with such different feelings about it. Ladislau found that he had a strange, warm glow when thinking about Charlotte and her failure to appreciate him. He had spent the day being fawned over by all these Welsh people who seldom met a Londoner, but this woman seemed uninterested. Why?

Charlotte had nothing but contempt for Ladislau after their meeting. She blamed him for all the bad coverage of sport on Channel 6 that she and her Dad had had to endure and now also she associated him with the loss of the playing field to Abacus. She knew that her views would not appear in a documentary, but that night she typed furiously away on a ten page analysis of all that was wrong with Channel 6's sports coverage. Her mother would have dragged her from her bedroom had she had the energy but Charlotte sat at the keyboard and typed angrily. Only when she had finished would she go downstairs and eat what had once been her dinner. It was worth having cold food to stand up for your beliefs.

Heather was tucked up on the sofa with Jon, the new boyfriend she had got in the supermarket. He was not the millionaire, billionaire or trillionaire that she had wanted five years ago. In fact, he was probably not even a thousandaire but he was decent and kind and that was what Heather needed. He probably knew that she would drop him like a hot pan if a millionaire did ever so much as look at her twice.

"Loser," she muttered for old time's sake as Charlotte walked past.

That Friday, as the staff of Abacus assembled to wish the TV crew team well as they left, Charlotte the Administrator strode forwards boldly and placed her report in Ladislau's hands. He placed it hurriedly in his briefcase and promised her that he would read it on the train. She doubted that she would ever hear from him again.

However, a week later, Charlotte's life took another odd turn and she moved a step closer to her destiny. She was sitting in the kitchen talking to her mother about making dinner while helping to sort through the bills. Her phone rang. It was not a number that she recognised, so she excused herself and went up to her room to answer.

"Hello Charlotte, this is Ladislau from Heron Productions."

That was a name that definitely did not deserve an EPICchat sound to accompany it.

"Hello."

"Charlotte, I really enjoyed your assessment of our sports coverage. I thought that you might tell me that things were a little staid or that Stacey's presenting was a little dull but you even went down to the angle of the sofa and the timing of the segments. You really know the show."

Of course I do, thought Charlotte, I have only been bonding with my Dad over it for years.

"I went to the production board with your audition tape too. You may not realise it but I am involved in quite a few sides of Channel 6's programming, not just documentaries."

"What audition tape?"

"The good news is that they really liked you, the spark, the enthusiasm - though they think that women's football may be something to look at in a separate programme, perhaps for next year's coverage."

"Great, I'm glad that you found my thoughts useful. I am about to attempt to make a kangaroo steak ratatouille so can you get to the point please?"

It was probably not kangaroo meat waiting to go into the frying pan, but it was from a cheap supermarket and that it was what it had said on the packet.

"We'd like to offer you a job with ... with certain conditions. Stacey has left us for lesser things and there is a vacancy. I suggested you."

"Me?"

"Yes, you."

Charlotte was frankly surprised and wondered what on earth Ladislau had in mind. She could hardly be expected to up and leave her life in Barry and go somewhere new.

"What conditions?"

"We need to do something with your look. We'll have a hair and beauty team work on you. You'll need to go blonde and I am sure that we can find you some leather trousers and accessories."

"For talking about football?"

"That's the style of the programme, men have makeovers too, so you cannot get me on sexism."

Charlotte felt distinctly uncomfortable with the thought that Ladislau was mentally dressing her as they spoke. She asked what else.

"We take you for a day's rehearsal and see how it goes. If that is okay then you get to present the next night. If that is okay, we will put together a month of hosting and promotional opportunities. Your contract will allow us to terminate the arrangement at any time. Oh yes, we'll pay you double what they're paying you at Abacus."

"All very well, but it's a hell of a commute from Barry."

"No-one can afford houses in London, so we put you up in one of our flats. The cost comes out of your wages but frankly it would cost more than your wages to find a house in London these days. Again, the moment we decide to sack you, you would lose all rights to it."

"Can I think about it?"

"Of course."

"I'll just put you on hold," said Charlotte, smiling at using a skill that she remembered from language lessons, though all she did was flip her phone on mute.

She needed to talk to her family. She walked downstairs and there were Heather and Jon cuddled up together on the sofa watching their favourite soap opera. It was best not to disturb them. In the kitchen, her mother was still surrounded by the bills. She could see her staring at them and she knew what she was thinking. It was not so much the money, it was the feeling that she had let everyone down. Somehow the health problems that she had been born with were stopping them enjoying their lives. She was not thinking about herself, she was thinking about being a burden on her daughters and her ex-husband. The light coming through the kitchen window was fading but, as it did so, it caught a glass bowl on the table and threw a strange set of shapes and patterns over her mother's tired face. Charlotte knew her answer at that moment.

"Are you still there, Ladislau?"

"I am. Look, if you're not sure, then we can add 3k to your salary, but don't push me further than that."

"I'll take the job."

"Good decision."

Charlotte looked around at her family and knew that she had to do it for them. On the other end of the phone, Ladislau contented himself that once again he had proven that people will do anything for money.

Charlotte hugged her mother and told her that everything was going to be all right. Then, assuring her that she really would start on the kangaroo steaks in a minute, Charlotte walked back up to her bedroom and fell into a crying heap on the bed.

Charlotte cried. She cried for the cruelty of the world, she cried for her mother feeling ashamed of being ill, she cried for not having her Dad in the house, she cried for having to leave home, she cried for living in a little house where she had to stick her head between the pillows in the middle of the night sometimes to block out the sound of the sister humping her boyfriend, she cried for the weight of it all that had built up over the years. Now it was possibly, tentatively, going to be lifted. She was going to be Charlotte the Sports Reporter. First thing tomorrow, she would buy some clear plastic folders to organise the information. Then she would ...

Charlotte smelt frying coming from downstairs. Her mother had started cooking. She leapt off the bed and ran downstairs. She could at least cook one meal before she left.

part three of four :

Charlotte the Sports Reporter

There were tears, guilt and fruitcake when Charlotte left on the next stage of her journey. There were her own tears of sadness about leaving, guilt from her Mam about 'sending her away' and then there were kind neighbours packing emergency homemade fruitcake into Charlotte's coat pockets 'in case they don't have proper food in London'.

Charlotte was amazed enough that someone would pay for her to travel to London by train, but she did notice that the Channel bought her a ticket valid for a return within a year so they were keeping their options open. Once in Cardiff, excitement started to build in her as she waited for the express train to London to be announced.

Once seated on the train, Charlotte watched out of the window as the geography of her world changed. She saw the eastern suburbs of Cardiff dissolve into the western suburbs of Newport and then it was under the Severn and into England. Unfamiliarity made the place names sound exotic to her – Bristol Parkway, Swindon, Didcot Parkway.

However, by the time that the train had reached Reading, a fear had settled in the bottom of her stomach. What was she actually doing? She was leaving Wales and crossing England to do what? People from Barry did not do this, especially girls. The likes of Mam, Dad, the sister and herself were born to live and die in Barry. Maybe this would only last a week and then things would go back to normal.

Thinking of her blonde sibling only made Charlotte more nervous. Ladislau had said that she would have to dye her hair blonde. Maybe it was like not wearing blue on television, maybe it clashed with the set? Charlotte allowed herself to believe for a moment that this was why all the women on television were blonde.

Her phone buzzed with a message –

POB LWC YN LLUNDAIN – REMEMBER, DO NOT ADVOCATE CAUTIOUS PLAY TOO MUCH. ALWAYS YOUR WEAKNESS. LOVE DAD XX

Charlotte laughed, he only ever used 'love' in text messages but it was always worth receiving. 'Pob lwc yn Llundain' – 'Good luck in London', that was also stretching Dad's Welsh too.

The message gave Charlotte the little boost of confidence and energy that she needed. She estimated that she had about half an hour between Reading and London Paddington and so she neatly unpacked her travel backpack and spread some of the documents on the table in front of her, along with some of the emergency fruitcake. Everything to do with her new flat was in a red plastic folder. She had included tickets from Paddington to the flat in Wandsworth, all paid for by Channel 6, and also a map of the area, marked with local shops, the train station and other points of use. Then there was a yellow folder - also clear plastic - which contained details of how to get from the flat to Channel 6 itself. This included a picture of the Channel 6 office building in Stratford and a few notes that she had made about the company. Finally, the green folder contained everything that Charlotte thought that she needed to know about London and her new life. She would jump off the train at Paddington, breathe in the polluted air and her new life would begin, at least for a week or two. She hoped that the new place had somewhere for her to put her folders.

It was an odd contrast. She told herself that this was only for a week or two but she had planned as if it were for a year or two.

* * * * *

Charlotte's first call in London was Channel 6 (yellow folder), where she picked up the key for her flat (red folder) and then headed there to settle in for the evening (red and green folders). She was under no illusions about the cost of the flat coming from her wages but it was only when she reached the building that she realised that her wages were not being very generous with her accommodation.

It was on the second floor of a building a few doors down from the overground station for Wandsworth Road. She pulled her suitcase up the stairs past peeling wallpaper and under a flickering light bulb, to the second floor where she would now live. As she struggled to find the key in her pocket, the automated lights went out.

"Welcome home," she muttered to herself.

To be fair, she had looked up property prices for the area and found that even this flat could sell for more than a whole terrace in Barry. It was a start, maybe as she made more money she would be able to afford somewhere that did not have carpet held together with duck tape on the communal stairs.

The inside was better. Wooden floors across three rooms – a decent-sized bedroom, a lounge (or front room as it would have been back home) and a modest kitchen. Channel 6 had it moderately furnished for her and there was a large TV screen on the wall bearing the message "Welcome to London, Charlotte, from all at Channel 6."

It reminded Charlotte of her first task. She opened her suitcase and took out a rolled-up poster and some blu-tac. With a little bit of struggling to stop it curling, she stuck it to the wall next to the television set. It was a photo taken from the hillier side of Barry looking down on the town, the docks, the Island and across the Severn Sea to Somerset. Charlotte smiled. Now she was home.

That evening was spent timing the walk to the station, assessing the local shops and then sorting her clothes into piles according to work, casual, style and colour combination. The Channel noted that they would dress her for appearing on screen, but still she chose a fairly smart outfit for her first day in her new role.

*   *   *   *   *

The next morning, Charlotte's excitement had to be sustained through a packed commuter train journey and then a twenty minute wait in Channel 6's airy and echo-y reception or 'atrium' as the signs had it. She introduced herself at the front desk as Channel 6's new sports reporter, but the receptionist told her bluntly that she would have to wait, whoever she was.

It was at this point that Charlotte realised that just opening her mouth in this place and hearing her Welsh accent identified her as someone who did not belong. The wait seemed to confirm it. Her excitement was now definitely anxiety.

Twenty minutes of anxious fretting and a little picking at a loose seam on her dress later, Charlotte saw two women enter the foyer. Both were tall and slim and both wore dark glasses and sparkly dresses. Had they not managed to go home after a night out or was this how people dressed in London?

One of them walked over to her, the clack clack clack of her high heels echoing through the atrium. She lowered her glasses and peered at Charlotte. Her eyes looked slightly tired but a smile played across her lips at the sight of the new recruit.

"You must be Charlotte the Welsh girl," she said, extending a gloved hand to be shaken.

Charlotte stood up slightly nervously and confirmed her identity.

"Tamsin," the woman said, "and that over there is Sarah, we are your beauty consultants. Welcome to Channel 6. Follow me."

Charlotte followed them, though she was convinced that the receptionist was sending her an evil stare as she did.

Behind the reception, the Channel 6 headquarters was a mass of corridors and doors that led in unexpected directions. Charlotte did see some signs that led to studios but she was already missing the familiarity of home. At least when they reached the hair and beauty room ('we call it the salon where dreams are made' – Tamsin) she recognised some of the tools of the trade.

Tamsin removed her glasses and looked Charlotte over like a sculptor surveying a block of unused marble. Without shades, Charlotte reckoned Tamsin to be older than Sarah by a good ten years or so.

"I can see what he sees in you," commented Sarah from across the room.

"Err ... thank you," said Charlotte awkwardly.

"Ah, frumpy teenager," said Tamsin slightly dismissively.

"What do you mean?"

"Frumpy teenager. Face it, as a teenager you were drab and dull and no-one fancied you. Now you are in your twenties, you have filled out a bit, got a bit of shape and definition to your body and you're pretty hot, but your first memories are still rejection so you don't ever really believe anyone who tells you that you look good."

Charlotte was not sure if she was supposed to agree or not.

"I did have a better looking younger sister," she said awkwardly.

"Ha! Didn't we all!" exclaimed Sarah, walking over, "But I'll bet that in her twenties she filled out in all the wrong places and suddenly found that boys had someone younger and cuter to lust after."

"I'm going to make myself a low calorie, sugar-free, fat-free, dairy-free, caffeine-free latte, if you want one," said Tamsin.

Charlotte smiled shyly, "A what?"

Sarah took over – "It's really a coffee-free coffee, it's much better for you than real coffee."

"Then why have it at all?"

"Oh, I couldn't go without my coffee in the morning!"

Charlotte returned to being quiet. She was out of her depth and wished that she had brought some emergency fruitcake with her. Tamsin and Sarah looked at her carefully, also not really used to a shy Welsh girl who did not say much. Having never been to Wales, they decided that all Welsh women were like this.

The room was arranged a little like the hairdressers that Charlotte used to visit back in Barry, only bigger and with more equipment. She sat in one of the seats and looked in the mirror. While Tamsin made coffee-free coffee, Sarah started to run her hands through Charlotte's hair.

"You know you're going blonde, don't you? That was a condition. And we have a whole new wardrobe for you. Basically, you'll need to come in the day before each programme for us to do your beauty and then for a few hours on the day. I know, it's rough, Danny will only be in here an hour before transmission at least."

"Danny – oh yes, the bloke with the waistcoats?"

"You've watched the show, then? Yes, your co-star. He'll always be on the left of you as people look at the screen. People read left to right so on television the man always has to go on the left to show that he is more important."

"Okay," said Charlotte collecting her thoughts, "I'm sorry if I'm a bit quiet, I'm nervous. I haven't been to London before, let alone TV studios. And they did say that I'm just on trial. You know, if I don't work out they won't let me actually go live or anything."

"Ah, innocent!" said Tamsin bringing over a tray with three coffee-free coffees, "That's probably part of your charm. No, they've ordered clothes in your size, they're expecting you here for at least a few months."

"Why?"

"Hey, we just make people look magnificent, we don't make those kind of decisions. Now – back to our business. We'll send you blonde. Then we'll take you through the wardrobe changes. We can probably pluck around the eyebrows a bit, big false lashes are a must and ... any chance we can put a bit of collagen in your lips?"

"No!" said Charlotte definitely, covering her lips with her hand.

"Okay, okay, we'll plump up the lips naturally with some bright red. We'll give you a full make-up make over before you go on screen each time."

"Okay," said Charlotte, partly just to feel as though she was in control of it in some way.

"Blonde first, then?" said Tamsin, sorting through the bottles on a table at the side of the room.

A thought struck Charlotte - they were turning her into Heather! She hated the thought and yet also she wanted to see a little of Heather's universe, so she lay back and relaxed. It felt odd being pampered. It felt unusual.

"I suppose that you had a very different upbringing to me," she said, "how often did you have meat as a teenager?"

Sarah and Tamsin moved to the back of the room to talk about this odd question. Neither could understand what she meant. Yes, there were beef sandwiches, pork chops, a lamb joint on a Sunday, roast duck in restaurants ... what on earth was she talking about? Sarah leaned in close to her colleague and suggested an answer.

"She must be talking about sex. You know, Welsh slang for sex or something. Maybe her cute sister was a bit of a slut and she is still jealous?"

Tamsin nodded and returned to preparing Charlotte's hair for colouring.

"Meat? Hardly ever, I didn't really have an exciting time as a teenager," she said.

"Ah, maybe we were not so different then. We hardly ever had it in my household, it just wasn't something you thought about. Well, not for me. My sister dreamed about having it with some rich man three times a day, but you know, that's just dreaming ..."

Sarah mouthed to Tamsin, "bit of a slut" and Tamsin nodded.

Charlotte's all day makeover, fuelled by energy drinks and coffee-free coffee for the most part, left her looking in the mirror at a different person. Her hair was now blonde and long thanks to dye and extensions. She had never worn quite so much make-up and they had styled her in a low-cut top with a bra designed for uplift. 'You have fabulously-shaped boobs' Tamsin had commented, 'but we need to push them around a bit. When on camera, lean forward too and our ratings will soar'. Then the contractually-obliged leather trousers were brought in. Charlotte stared at the person in the mirror.

"What's wrong? Not good?" asked Tamsin, perhaps aware that she was dealing with Channel 6's new presenting talent as much as a quiet girl from Wales.

"No ... it's ... I've never seen myself like this before," said Charlotte and then turned her head sideways and blew the mirror a full-lipped kiss, "I do look a bit like one of those blonde bimbos you see on TV shows."

"Congratulations Charlotte, you've got the job!" joked Sarah, to much laughter from her partner in beauty.

The next day was the rehearsal. The Channel wanted to see how Danny and Charlotte worked on screen together and sure enough, an hour before rehearsal started, Danny appeared. Something told Charlotte that he had not received evil looks from the receptionist.

Of course, Charlotte recognised him from watching the show, but Danny seemed somehow smaller in person. He was already dressed in a smart grey waistcoat and trousers and she noticed that all the attention that he really needed was a slight trim to his beard and a new pair of shoes. Heather used to get more of a makeover from their mother before she left for school each morning, she thought.

While the make-up team fussed about the gel in Danny's hair, he explained the show to her.

"Basically, we're only there to link the highlights packages and do some quick interviews. There's a list of guests, we've usually got an ex-pro and a Manager."

"I used to watch the show with my Dad."

"Ah well, there you go. Talk to the camera as if you are talking directly to your Dad. The autocue will do your script and really it is that simple."

"That sounds easy."

"Oh and have you got your gym card?"

"No, I ... what card?"

"I'll get it sorted out for you. You now have membership of a chain of gyms, you'll find in your contract that you have to follow the company workout several times a week."

"Really?"

"Of course, they employ you, they can ask anything of you. You could be sacked for anything that brings the Channel into disrepute – not looking fit and healthy would be included in that."

The make-up team had finished trimming Danny's beard and giving him the make-up for being under television lights. Charlotte thought that he did have a natural 'blokeish' air that came across on television. She would try to copy that natural feel herself, even if she did not look like herself.

"When do we watch the matches?" she asked.

"Matches?" answered Danny, sizing up his trimmed beard in the mirror while Sarah giggled behind him, "Oh no, we don't watch any – well, on a Saturday we'll be too busy in the studio for a start. I suppose that you could take in a midweek game if you wanted. Get the Channel to message the clubs and they'll send over tickets."

Charlotte watched her eyes widen in the mirror. Money really could buy happiness. Imagine how pleased her Dad would be when free tickets to football matches arrived in the post!

The studio itself was smaller than she had thought that it would be but she found her place sitting to the right of Danny on the sofa. Charlotte became aware of the sound of the director's voice coming from the studio gallery via a radio microphone in her ear. Orders would come through to them – 'Danny, ask a question about tactics', 'Charlotte- smile more', 'Danny, do the link to the next segment', 'Charlotte – don't look so nervous when you smile'.

She was nervous too. There were the occasional fluffed lines, but Danny covered for them well. He seemed to grow in size under the television lights and that blokeish charm carried into the studio unrattled.

"What happened to the last female presenter?" Charlotte asked in a break between rehearsing segments.

"Oh, Stacey went to work for a jewellery sales channel. We've still got links. Do them a guest appearance and they'll probably give you some free rings or necklaces. Work those personal appearances for all the freebies you can get."

Charlotte smiled to herself as she realised that she had birthday and Christmas presents for the sister sorted out now.

The voice returned to her ear - "And we're going to tape the next section for review overnight. Follow the autocue and imagine it's for real. Going to tape now in four, three, two, one ..."

The theme music started and Danny was soon smiling directly at the camera as he told the non-existent viewers about what a great show was lined up for them. She followed his lead and the studio gallery made appreciative comments in her ear.

"They're pleased," said Danny at the end of it, "there's life before the jewellery channel for you yet!"

Charlotte give him a hug, which seemed to surprise him, and felt contented with her performance. She still felt like a visitor from an alien planet, but she could see herself blending in with the humans now.

"See you tomorrow," said Danny, before adding, "you should be able to pick up your gym card from reception – you know how the song goes, keep young and beautiful, if you want to be employed! Don't mean to freak you out, but Ladislau himself is directing our first show!"

Charlotte looked around as people started to pack up. It struck her how alone she was on this new adventure. Danny was off to do whatever he did in the evenings, her beauty team were now part of the beauty team for what sounded like a taping of a pro-celebrity cheese blending show and she knew no-one else in the city.

Ideally, she would now pick up her gym card and start on her personal training plan. However, Charlotte was no ideal. She picked up her gym card all right, but also knew that in her green folder was the address of the nearest take away pizza place. An evening in front of the big TV, eating pizza and messaging her family seemed more interesting. The Channel could own her tomorrow, tonight she was not going to do what she was told.

*   *   *   *   *

The next day Charlotte was in early for the start of her transformation. The blonde Charlotte in the mirror still looked strange to her, but she liked the way that the beauty team attended to the bags under her eyes and the crumpled look she had gained from falling asleep on the sofa around two in the morning. The more she protested that it was not due to a night of wild clubbing, the more Tamsin and Sarah believed that they had a party girl on their hands ("always the quiet ones," muttered Sarah while Tamsin nodded sagely).

Danny arrived a lot later in the day for his minor makeover. He reminded her to become used to the sound of Ladislau's voice in her ear and that it was rare that he directed the programme. She knew that she was being watched. What Charlotte did not realise was that the rest of the crew had been given an extensive list of ways to save the occasion for when she dried up, had stage fright or otherwise messed up.

Once in the studio, Danny welcomed the viewers and introduced the first match, a recording of Manchester United playing Aston Villa in one of the Premier League's overseas matches in Boston. Charlotte had never liked the overseas matches, but then the Premier League was a global product.

During the coverage, a middle-aged man with greying hair on his temples and wearing a slightly battered suit entered the studio and sat on the sofa next to them.

"Simon!" said Danny and jumped up to shake his hand.

Charlotte recognised him as the former Manager of Stoke City, sacked after a poor run of results and costly dealings in the transfer market. He was a regular pundit now and certainly seemed chummy with Danny. He kissed her hand rather unnecessarily and wished her well on her first show. Ladislau was telling them to sit down as they were going to tape the reactions.

"A good day at the office for Man U or a bad defending display from Villa?" asked Danny.

"Well ...," started Simon, "Man U will be happy with that and think of it as a comfortable win, but I think that the Villa manager will be unhappy with the nature of the goals."

"You've picked out some moments where you think that Villa's back line fell asleep?"

"Yes ..."

Charlotte tuned out for a moment, while keeping her face in the same permanent smile that the viewers would want to see. The pundit was explaining the defensive line and how it was sitting too deep at crucial moments. She looked ahead on the autocue and saw that her first line was about whether Simon was enjoying his time on the golf course. She decided to go off script.

"So Simon," said Charlotte when they reached her line, "why do you think Villa played such a tight team? They could see that Man U were effectively playing wingers and yet they did nothing to stop themselves being stretched wider?"

There was a quiet panic in the studio gallery, Simon looked to Danny for re-assurance, but he was nodding at him to reply.

"It's a good question, Charlotte," he said with a touch of surprise that annoyed her, "I do think that there was a certain tactical naïvety from the Manager on that one."

"And are you enjoying your time on the golf course now?"

There was a chuckle from the pundit and a note of relief in the studio gallery as the pundit explained that his handicap was doing well but that his wife was looking forward to him getting back to work. Danny introduced the next highlights.

Ladislau's voice was strong and clear in Charlotte's ear – "You stick to the script. Do not ask additional questions. Tactics will be discussed by Danny."

"It was a good question actually," noted Simon thoughtfully, "I do think that Villa didn't really think it through properly. I wasn't going to get into that on air or no club will give me another job. Loyalty to the profession and all that."

"I'm sorry Ladislau," lied Charlotte.

In the studio gallery there was some discussion.

"Are you sure about her?" one of the technicians asked Ladislau.

"Oh yes, she's a diva that's all, thinks she knows things. It's good though, the fans will find her sparky and enthusiastic. We never got that from the last one. Keep her to the script and she may last."

* * * * *

Charlotte grew in confidence as she came to know Tamsin and Sarah better. There were other make-up artists and hair and beauty technicians who occasionally helped out, but the two of them had been allocated as 'hers'.

Charlotte estimated that Tamsin was in her forties but with a lot of beauty treatments and the odd bit of surgery. She had been to the local beauty school in Guildford and trained for the role, moving up through local television into national channels and finally Channel 6. Sarah had been to the same school and started as Tamsin's apprentice. They were remarkably in tune and trusted with most of the Channel 6 'stars'. They both said that they rated Charlotte as more interesting than their usual clients, though this was partly the exotic strangeness of someone from Wales.

They also both fancied Danny. That was clear from how they both made jokes about him and speculated about his social life. The man himself was not averse to winking and flirting with them, but then he always had a broad smile for everyone.

Charlotte stuck to the script in every way after her first appearance. She kept her appointments at the gym and made personal and promotional appearances with help from Tamsin and Sarah's makeovers. When her pay cheque came through, she sent a good amount home to Mam and always included gifts for Heather and tickets to Cardiff City matches for Dad. Talk of her being sacked if she did not make a good impression each week was soon forgotten. She had made the right hand side of the Channel 6 sports presentation sofa hers in a very short space of time.

Charlotte's neighbourhood was hardly glamorous, but she got to know the man in the local shop and a few of the local people. The overground train to work was no hassle and she watched the changing billboards by the station with interest. There was the same 'Oh, I could not do without my coffee in the morning!' poster that had been up in Barry for years but the other posters were for banks, sports cars, gold watches ... things that were never advertised back home.

Then again, she would never have afforded membership of a gym before. Now she had an ex-army personal trainer who would surround her with jelly babies and then make her exercise amid their smell without letting her eat any. She missed home and went back to see Mam, Heather and Dad in-between tapings a couple of times. Heather had started to move her things into Charlotte's old room, which caused arguments.

It was in the run-up to Christmas that Charlotte decided to do something about the isolation of London life. It was time to get to know her co-presenter a little better. He was charming, good-looking, fun to be around and supportive, even letting her ask some slightly more challenging questions on air when he could. Casually after broadcast one day she asked him about whether they might go for a drink somewhere and he said how about she went over to his apartment for some home cooking? She said yes, of course. Later when she asked Tamsin and Sarah if they would give her a makeover for it 'off the books', they said 'yes, of course' too.

"Is it a date, then?" asked Tamsin, looking through some of the Channel's accessories for presenters.

"I don't really know. I asked if he would 'go for a drink', he said would I go over to his – that's positive, right?"

"Yes ..."

Sarah walked over to the accessories shelves and whispered to Tamsin, "She asked him out – is that a Welsh thing?" to which her partner in beauty replied, "Remember what we know about her sister, it must be a Welsh thing!"

"What are you two whispering about?"

"Just your accessory choices. I think that we are going classy with this. He hasn't seen you like that, it'll impress him," said Tamsin with a smile.

"How's your sister these days?" asked Sarah, though it seemed a jump in conversation to Charlotte.

"I was back home in Barrybados a couple of weeks ago. They say they miss me but Dad is so proud, seeing his girl on telly. Mam seems to be a bit better now and did I tell you about Heather's boyfriend Jon? They're moving on, I suppose."

Tamsin came round and stood in front of Charlotte.

"You listen to me now," she said, "you shouldn't be having a first date in a private place. That's such bad personal safety. I don't care how well you think that you know him - I am going to take your number and you are to have mine - if you haven't called me by midnight then I will send the police. Right?"

Charlotte agreed sheepishly and passed her phone over for the number to be copied. Tamsin was right, a meeting at someone's apartment sounded like dropping in as a friend rather than a place for a first date. She sat back and waited for the transformation.

*   *   *   *   *

It was later that evening that Charlotte realised that she had a flat but Danny had an apartment. There was a definite difference. Maybe the Channel put their better talent closer to the studio, maybe you had to work your way up from Wandsworth Road to Stratford. Whatever the reason, he had a lovely open-plan sitting and dining room with a kitchen made out of a corner of it. There was a run of bedrooms hidden to one side.

Danny had been cooking and the aroma filled the place. He took her coat and her bag and gave her a glass of wine. Charlotte looked at her phone - she had four hours before she turned into a pumpkin or before Tamsin phoned.

Charlotte let Danny talk about himself. It turned out that he had grown up around television, his father was a documentary maker and he had been to a film school in East London. He resisted questions about his teenage years (Charlotte wanted to know if he could be classed as a 'frumpy teenager') by finishing off the cooking of the chicken stir fry.

"And your love of football?" asked Charlotte, leaning back on the sofa while he cooked.

"Well, it was growing up around it too. I've always been a supporter. I did a few minor presenting things for Channel 6 and then when they bought the rights for the Premier League highlights, I had to do it."

"You're a little wedded to the long ball game, if I may say."

"I'm what?"

There was an awkward silence while he served the food and poured some more wine into Charlotte's glass. He was not used to a woman telling him that he was wrong about something, it was simply something that did not happen in television. Was it because she was Welsh?

"I suppose so," he admitted at length, "and you know more about football than most women I have met."

"I am not like most women you have met," replied Charlotte with a flirtatious giggle.

"No, I mean it. Look, I know years ago they had this thing about equality and everything, but you see how the world is now. We men are expected to know things, take the lead and so on. Yet when I am talking every week, I can see when you are itching to get in with a comment on the play or the tactics."

"I used to watch the football with Dad, it was easy to learn."

There was something about Danny that Charlotte could not quite work out. She was sure that there was something that he was not telling her, but her interview skills were too new to work it out. The wine tasted good, the meal was good, the conversation flowed and Charlotte felt like there was a time when she should make a move.

Their conversation was mostly idle chit chat. Danny wanted to know about what life had been like in Barry for Charlotte and she asked him about his own upbringing and where he bought his waistcoats. She was trying to be cute and funny and there seemed to be plenty of smiling and gentle laughter to persuade her that she was doing well at this.

Once the meal was done and Danny had removed the plates to the dishwasher (Charlotte's mother would not have been impressed to know that her daughter still did not have the skills - or rather the inclination- to help do this), they sat together on the sofa to finish off their wine. It was there that Charlotte made her move. She sidled over to Danny and, with a heart pounding with anxiety, kissed him firmly on the lips.

"Ugh!" he yelled, pushing her away from him.

Men should learn that when a woman tries to kiss them, the correct response is never 'ugh!'. Even if you follow up with 'Oh God, I'm so sorry!' as Danny did, the woman will be running for the door as Charlotte did.

She had her coat and her bag and she fumbled with both as she ran down the stairs of the apartment, the sound of Danny shouting her name after her. It was before eleven o'clock but, coughing on tears of embarrassment, she phoned her safe call.

"Tamsin, I ..."

"Charlotte ... what's wrong?"

It sounded very loud wherever Tamsin was, she was shouting over screaming and music.

"I'm safe, look ... I ... don't worry."

"Where are you?"

"I'm outside Danny's apartment in Stratford, I'll find a taxi ..."

"Nonsense, I'll send a taxi to get you. I know his area. Stand somewhere in public and when the driver arrives he'll have my card and my signature on the back of it. Don't get in a taxi if the driver doesn't have that, okay?"

"Okay ... but I ..."

"Nonsense, you're coming with us. We're out with the Beautiful People and you belong here too."

"What? I'm not dressed for clubs and bars, you'll be all glittery and I just don't feel like anything but a fool."

The background sound was dying down now as Tamsin had reached the outer door of wherever she was and was asking about taxis.

"I keep saying nonsense. It doesn't matter. We'll tell people that Welsh girls always dress for a date when they go for a night out. No-one here's been to Wales, they'll never know."

Charlotte really wanted to go home and cry while wondering why she had been such an idiot. However, Tamsin's mothering ways made her feel safe and cared for in a city where she felt that she knew no-one.

When the taxi delivered her to a club somewhere on the other side of the city, Tamsin was waiting and paid the driver. Before they went in, she asked Charlotte two questions - 'do you want to get drunk?' and 'do you want to get laid?'

Charlotte replied that she was okay with the first one, indeed she was well on the way to the first one, but she wanted to avoid the second one. Tamsin put a protective arm around her and told her that she would make sure that however drunk she got, she would not have to worry about stupid, drunken mistakes. Charlotte wanted to say that she had made one mistake that night already but asked something else instead.

"Why are you doing this for me? What do you get out of it?"

Tamsin lowered her shades and gave Charlotte a serious look, "I've been doing this job for a long time now and I have seen too many young women like you getting in trouble. You know it's a sexist world, but that doesn't mean we can't look out for each other."

It occurred to Charlotte that not everyone thought that everything was about money. They were rare but they existed.

Charlotte's night from that point onwards was a mix of noise, music and sound. A lot of things spun. She was introduced to so many people and she heard, 'you're from Wales, how exotic!' or 'you're the new girl from the sports show!' so often that she just politely nodded. The music was too loud for much conversation anyway. The Beauty crowd covered her bar bill for the night and she found tequila, whisky, vodka and some bright-red cocktails coming her way at a steady speed. She danced, oh she danced a lot, one mad thought being to burn off the alcohol with dancing but somehow, somewhere her night spun and spun and spun until she was waking up in the dark at four in the morning.

Charlotte had time to realise that she was lying down on a sofa and to lean over the side of it, before she was violently sick into a bucket placed strategically there. It was her flat. She was in the recovery position - thank goodness, fully-clothed but for her shoes discarded somewhere - and she was vomiting into a bucket. She blacked out again just as she started to think "But I don't own a bucket!"

*   *   *   *   *

Charlotte would never dwell on quite how rough she felt the next day or indeed the day after that. Tamsin re-arranged Charlotte's schedule at work so as not to risk the Channel sacking her for being sick, a real danger with companies looking to preserve their profits. Danny was also helpful for some reason, although the make-up team dealt with him frostily. Indeed, when Charlotte did return to work she found that all the beauty department were keen to work with her as one of the few presenters who were interested in them. Apparently, she had done tequila shots with Margaret while listening to the whole story of her bitter divorce and this had earned approval among many. Margaret said that Charlotte had given her 'the best advice of my damn life'. Charlotte did not remember it.

She now had friendly 'hellos' as she walked the corridors at Channel 6. She thanked Tamsin effusively but never received anything other than a casual 'any time'.

Danny tried to apologise but Charlotte lied to him and said that it was all forgotten. There was something slightly lacking in their on-screen chemistry from then on however and she had to remember to fake her chuminess with him every broadcast.

It was only as the office Christmas Party approached that Danny finally managed to have a moment alone with Charlotte. The make-up team were briefly called away for a hair emergency on a fishing show and Danny took his moment to talk to her.

"Look, you know how sorry I am about what happened, but I can explain," he said quickly from his make-up chair.

Charlotte stared straight ahead into the mirror and replied, "I don't need an explanation."

"I reacted really badly, I'm sorry, it's just ... there's something I need to tell you, but it has to be in private, not here. Please, please, please come over again, I can explain."

"Give you the chance to humiliate me again, then? Why am I thinking 'no' is a good answer here?"

"Our ratings are starting to drop, there's talk about new presenters, ask Ladislau."

"I don't care about the ratings," replied Charlotte, though she knew that a steady stream of income for her family was making a big difference.

"I know, I know, you want to do a good job," said Danny in a low whisper, "that's why it's even more important that I talk to you. You understand that it's not about money!"

At that point, Sarah re-entered the room, tutting about how the fishing show just could not expect to work with air and water and yet keep perfect make-up. Oh and the oh-so-vain presenter woman thought that standing next to a salmon made her look pink. Tamsin was still there doing make-up for the salmon.

Danny and Charlotte stared straight ahead, avoiding eye contact. Sarah would work around them both without realising that anything was wrong.

Danny found other moments to ask the same question and each time Charlotte was dismissive. She told herself that there was nothing that he could say that would make her change her mind.

Then one day he whispered, "It won't be just you and me, my boyfriend will be there."

That changed her mind.

* * * * *

Charlotte let Danny take her coat and had a brief flashback to her previous humiliation. This time though she had not dared to tell the beauty team where she was going. Once again there was a strong cooking smell wafting throughout the apartment but the crucial difference was that the table was set for three this time. Danny returned to behind the kitchen bar to check on his vegetables.

"Glass of wine?" he asked.

"Oh go on then, it'll only help when I do try to throw myself at you again."

"Ed! Wine needed!"

A tall, smartly-dressed man with a shock of red hair emerged from one of the back rooms and gave Charlotte a smile and then an unexpected hug.

"You must be Charlotte the Sports Presenter! You're as cute as he says!"

"Oh nonsense, it's all down to the hair and beauty team."

Ed walked over to Danny and gave him an ostentatious kiss on the cheek, "Well, hands off, he's mine!"

Sometimes when you know someone, you think that you know everything about them. Then you see them with the person who they love and suddenly you realise what has been missing from your impression of them. Around Ed, Danny was a little less rougher around the edges, a touch quieter, but so clearly in love that less needed to be said. Charlotte started to forget her embarrassment over her last visit and warmed to Ed.

"He's poaching the salmon with a touch of white, but I think that we should open something a little more drinkable. Here –I found this for you, Welsh Girl."

Ed passed Charlotte a bottle of Glyndwr Wine, the label saying that it was made in Llanbethian, not far from Barry. She nodded as if she knew what she was doing and passed it back to Ed.

"Not a wine fan? No worries, it's not all bad. Climate change has pushed the wine growing regions further north. The south of Wales is apparently quite good – not that I've been, well, who can afford to travel these days?"

"Ignore him," said Danny, looking up from his boiling pans, "he's trying to be impressive. He works in an architect's office."

"Oh! Getting competitive now, are we? You're the one who spent her last visit trying to get into her knickers!"

Charlotte started coughing as she tried to restrain herself from laughing out loud. Ed shook his head and opened the wine for the three of them. Handing Charlotte a glass, he gave her a conspiratorial wink.

Ed and Charlotte went to the dining table and sat down while Danny finished the cooking.

"So, tell me, do this hair and make-up team do your clothes as well?" asked Ed.

"They even shave her legs for her!" called Danny from across the room.

"Hush, wish they would pay a bit more attention to him. I like your dress by the way."

"Thank you, I am a Channel 6 product, they do have to look after me. You have a nice style yourself and I do sometimes shave my own legs."

"Nonsense, why do that, if they'll do it for free! Wish I could get that kind of service, just don't get that same level of freebies in architecture."

Danny arrived at the table carrying two plates of food and put them down in front of them. As he did so, he addressed Charlotte with the seeming non-sequitur, "How do I know that you are not a spy?"

"What?"

"You know how it is," added Ed, a little joviality gone from his voice, "there's people taking account of your every move. There's a big office in Cheltenham where they keep a record of everything you do."

Danny returned with the third plate and his glass of wine, "Everything you do online, every phone call you make, the CCTV cameras in every street, you are being tracked."

"Well, I know that! It's for our security. Terrorists are trying to kill us!"

Danny and Ed exchanged a look. They looked as though they shared a secret world and Danny wanted to offer Charlotte a key to part of it. First though, there was a pause so that the three of them could start eating their salmon. It was good. Charlotte reflected that the wealthy could afford good food and this made them even healthier so they spent less on hospital bills and as a result this made them even wealthier and so they could afford good food ... and so on.

"It's good food," said Charlotte.

"Compliments to the chef," added Ed, raising his glass of wine.

"Thank you, glad you like it. Charlotte, I know you're not a spy."

"That's a ... compliment?"

"It is. Think about my file in Cheltenham, it's going to have front and centre that I am gay."

Ed mouthed at Charlotte "he is, you know" and she laughed.

"Usually he says 'well, you never told me!' and storms out," said Danny.

Charlotte was enjoying their rapport. They had clearly been together a long time and had all those set ways of behaving and interacting that all the most loving couples develop.

"Okay, okay, look ... my file will say that I am gay. Channel 6 don't want people to know that, my agent doesn't want people to know that. No-one should know it if I want to continue my career. It is something perfect to blackmail me with."

"Oh come on, it's 2046," replied Charlotte, taking a large slurp of wine while she talked, "no-one worries about that now. There are lots of gay people on TV, on the internet, in politics ... even in architect's offices!"

Ed raised his glass and touched it to Charlotte's gently. Then he refilled both of them.

"Yes, but football is still ... some parts of television. Look, imagine if you tried to go on air dressed in tracksuit bottoms and an old paint-splattered jumper."

"You'd rock it, darling," added Ed re-assuringly.

"You wouldn't do it, it's not your role. And that's my point, people don't want me to be gay, so I can't be. It's more than that though – Ed could have made a great wine-taster ... just like you are clearly intelligent but never get to use it."

Charlotte shook her head, "That's just the way of life. We all have things we're interested in, sure but we need to make money somehow. And what do you mean I'm intelligent? I am, but ..."

"You know it as well as I do. Yet, you know how the Channel sets it up. If next week Big Doug from Bolton Wanderers is on the show, I will ask him about why his team is playing the long ball game so much this season, you will ask him about whether he's heard the gossip about what his midfielders got up to in an all-night bar last week."

"It's sexist, I grasped that when I was told that I had to dye my hair blonde. That's TV, that's society. You do what you do ..."

"To earn enough money to pay your mother's hospital bills," added Ed with a note of sadness in his voice.

Charlotte did not react immediately. Instead, she finished her food, drank her wine and pouted at her dining companions. She wanted to disagree with them, but she also had the image of her file in Cheltenham, probably not as well colour-coded and labelled as she would have made it, showing that she could be exploited because of her mother's health.

Danny placed his hand on hers and she pulled it away from him. For someone on television every week, she was still intensely private about her family.

"Why are you telling me all this?"

Ed reached over and placed a hand on top of hers. This time she did not pull away.

"Because there is another way," said Ed with a smile.

The three of them finished the meal with no more than idle chit-chat about the weather, broadcasting, the vanity of architects and plans for the weekend. This time, Charlotte remembered that she was not at home but a guest in someone else's home and so offered to help wash up. Ed said that Channel 6 would never stand for Charlotte's soft hands doing manual labour and that she could leave Danny to load the dishwasher.

"Tell me about this other way, then," she said as they sat back down across a pair of matching sofas, Ed having chosen another bottle of wine for them.

Danny leant forward and looked earnest. This was unlike the sincerity that he showed on air when he was saying something like, "And that was a troubling result for fans of Doncaster Rovers."

"There are people out there who do things for nothing. Rather, no money, they do them for the love of doing them."

"What do you mean?"

"I mean that not everyone thinks that money is all that matters."

"You're making no sense. Money makes the world go round, we all know that. We have to earn or what would we do?"

"Enjoy ourselves?" asked Ed.

Charlotte was frowning and looking puzzled. No-one had ever said to her before that anything mattered more than money.

"There's an underground movement called 'the third sector' or sometimes 'the voluntary sector'. They're a small group of people who do things differently."

Ed interrupted his partner with a more enthusiastic delivery, "they have a thing called 'volunteering'".

"Oh, I've heard of that!" said Charlotte contemptuously, "If you don't have any work, you have to log on to the Job Centre Plus website and they send you details of somewhere to go and volunteer or it's against the law. Everyone hates it."

"No Charlotte," said Ed slowly, "people choose to do it, people do it to help."

They drank their wine in a hesitant silence, the two men wondering if she would be convinced, Charlotte not really knowing what to believe but feeling as though there was something about the help that she sent her family that suggested that she knew that money was not everything in life.

"How do you know about this fourth sector then?" she asked after pondering and drinking.

"Third sector," corrected Danny, "because when I was coming out, it was difficult."

Ed put his hand in Danny's but added sarcastically, "The poor lamb, he had no idea. I was queer as a daffodil from before I knew what a daffodil was, but he had 'the struggle'."

Danny continued undeterred, "I was confused. I had a girlfriend, I was trying to work out who I was and why

I fancied all the same actors that she did. Someone passed me a number for something called the LGBT Centre of Excellence."

"They make us all into excellent lesbians, gay, bisexual and transgender people. Before we were just plain ordinary," added Ed.

Danny was clearly used to the running commentary on the story and ignored it, "They were a great helpline. It just felt so good to have someone to talk to, you know."

"I know that kind of thing though," said Charlotte, "it's like the Pepsico Befrienders, you can talk to them about anything at a reduced rate from standard networks."

"No, it was free. Everyone there volunteered. Not forced by the Job Centre Plus Website either, just wanting to help other people, it was extraordinary. It opened my eyes and I wanted to do the same."

"Can I visit them?"

Danny shook his head sadly, "They were shut down by government enforcement officers a few years ago. No-one likes the third sector, it undermines the narrative that the only thing that matters in life is making money, it's a threat. That's why I needed to know if you're a spy."

Charlotte drank her wine and allowed Ed to give her a refill. The well-decorated apartment started to swim in front of her a little and she was not sure if it was the affect of the wine or what she was hearing.

"What are you doing about it?" she asked finally.

Ed threw his hands in the air as a sign of an exasperation long-held.

"Don't mind him, he despairs of me sometimes," said Danny.

"I despair of him sometimes," came the confirmation from Ed.

"I'm not brave enough. I had a pretty decent upbringing and a career in sport is pretty safe for now. There'll always be football. I want to help but ... I don't know where to start. You just ... you just do, I think. You're a rare person, you've actually come a long way, I think that you have a view of how far everyone could come."

Charlotte shook her head. She wanted to say that even if this were true, she did not know where to start or what to do – was there even a plan, a chart, a to do list?

"Ed phoned some people claiming to be your agent ..."

"He what? You what?"

"My rates are very competitive."

"If you want to take it, there's an advert booked for you to do at Harrison's Carpets in Neath on Monday. No-one at the Channel will think anything odd if you say that you want to spend a little time with your family around it."

"Barry isn't that near Neath," said Charlotte.

"Number of people who know where Barry is? Number of people who care where Barry is? You're not dealing with anyone who handles a map other than when it's telling their car where to drive. I've also got a card for you."

Danny passed over a small rectangle of card. Charlotte made a move to take it but Danny snatched it back at the last minute.

"Remember, the third sector is an underground movement. If the Channel found out you were involved with a group so radical, if anyone found out ... it would be the end of your career here. Think about it before taking the card."

Charlotte grabbed the card, feeling as though being warned was not really important to her. The card was blank on one side and on the other read, '8 Orchard'.

Ed took over the instructions, "Go to Orchard House in Swansea and ask for Room 8. They'll be expecting you an hour or so after your advert shoot. You might want to disguise yourself a little, but ... that's the nearest contact I could find for you."

"8 Orchard?" asked Charlotte with disbelief, "That is your code for Room 8 in Orchard House? You're clearly not the organisational genius behind this movement!"

"Think about it. Tell no-one. Other than me, obviously. If you do go there, tell me."

Charlotte felt overwhelmed by all this information. It appealed to her, of course, the idea that not everyone was motivated by money. She knew that already in some ways – not just her family but how Tamsin had looked after her on the night out... she knew that it was possible. Everything she had learned told her that it was not the natural way though.

"Can we talk about something else? You're pickling my head," she said.

Ed was straight on to the case with music to dance to and a race to finish the wine. Danny sat back and watched. Charlotte patted him on the head and asked him to look after her shoes while she danced. For a little while they forgot about the serious conversation.

Ed could probably have continued drinking wine, dancing and chatting until three in the morning, but Danny was tiring and told them that it was time for Charlotte's big exit.

"Big exit?" she asked.

"I've got a photographer waiting outside to take pictures of you when you leave and sell them to the 'papers, online 'blogs or whatever."

"Why?"

"It's in keeping with the story. If you have to spend a few days in Wales, they'll think that your world has been thrown into turmoil by events tonight. You're a minor celebrity, use the cover."

Charlotte sighed and started to collect her things. She fitted back into her shoes, zipped up her bag and reached for her coat.

"Coat over the arm," said Ed.

"What?"

"Here's what I suggest – coat over the arm, ruffle up your hair, the back of your head especially, pull yourself round a bit inside your dress as if you had to put it on in a hurry and it didn't quite fit right. That's it – bra strap showing definitely."

"And when you leave," added Danny, "pause long enough for our man to take the photo and then hurry off looking shame-faced and guilty."

"Why?" asked Charlotte, who had been adjusting her dress as directed at this point.

"Ah, the innocence!" sighed Ed, looking skywards.

"No, I know 'why' as in what I am trying to say went on here. I know what I am pretending went on here but why have I got anything to be shame-faced about if what we are pretending went on, actually went on?"

Danny and Ed exchanged glances and Danny simply said, "It's what society expects. You're a woman leaving a man's house at three in the morning, you should be ashamed."

Charlotte draped her coat over her arm and spoke to no-one in particular as she did so, "It's all wrong though, the hiding everything. You two – you're a bloody good couple, why should you have to hide it? Why should I be embarrassed about what went on here or what I am pretending went on here rather? No-one expects that of you in this story we're selling! Why must people always try to be what they are not?"

Ed hugged her unexpectedly and Danny patted him on the back as he did so.

"That's the way society is, Charlotte," he said.

Ed looked at her straight in the face and added, "And that's why you are the one to make it different."

part four of four :

Charlotte the Liberator

Returning to Wales felt like snuggling up in a warm duvet on a cold winter's night. The cost of petrol and the fares charged by the bus and train companies might have made travel rare for most, but Charlotte had read about people cheering as they approached the 'Croeso i Gymru' sign on the M4 or when the train emerged from the Severn Tunnel into the broad, bright sunlight of South Wales.

Charlotte missed Wales. She liked London well enough, but it was a place where she was always on display. Although she did manage to sneak out occasionally in disguise, she was mostly expected to be a glamorous woman around town, an ambassador for her TV channel's brand and left in no doubt that her wage was a payment they made to take her privacy from her.

Back in Wales, she could throw on her favourite clothes and just relax and be herself. She was looking forward to being herself. It was little things really – she spent most of her public appearance days in high-heeled shoes now and so going about in flat shoes was a change. Someone had once claimed that Welsh people were shorter than people in London, but she had a theory that the reason that Welsh women tended to be three or four inches shorter than London women was that they just had more sensible shoes.

As soon as the train emerged from the Severn Tunnel, her smile broadened as she saw the fields of her homeland. Rushing through the first stations, she looked out of the train window and saw 'Caldicot / Cil-y-Coed'. It would sound odd to someone from outside Wales, but there was something so peculiar about places in England with their one place name per sign. This was back to normal.

Charlotte had applied more make-up and changed into more celebrity-like clothes by the time that she reached Neath. Peter the Carpet Man was simply delighted that she had agreed to take part in his marketing scheme. Her 'agent' had told him that she liked to take an interest in local companies and although he had never heard of this before, he was grateful for publicity. He was older and had a slightly cheaper suit than Charlotte had expected. There must be something about carpet sales that did not provide a good living or maybe she had just been in London too long and become accustomed to wealth.

"We are so, so pleased to have you here," he said, meeting her at Neath station, "have you been to Neath before?"

Charlotte put her suitcase in front of him for him to take without thinking about it. She winced at being rude but she had learned what was expected of even a minor celebrity. She said that no, this was her first visit to the town.

"Very good, very good," he said, rubbing his hands together before straining to lift her case, "my car is just over here. Good journey, I hope."

"Good to be back in Wales," said Charlotte truthfully and Peter the Carpet Man nodded enthusiastically.

It was a simple job. Harrison Carpets was a vast showroom of carpet rolls and Charlotte was to take various photos with a leg placed triumphantly on a carpet or against the backdrop of carpets hanging from the walls. There was a photographer who shouted occasional commands, including the frankly bizarre 'Grab the carpet beater and really spank that carpet!' but they both knew that there was not much variety to be had on this job.

"You don't mind if we touch you up later, do you?" asked the photographer during a break.

"You know how it works," replied Charlotte, surprising herself a little with how world-weary she sounded.

"He's going to ... what?" asked Peter with a hint of nervous excitement.

"Touch up my photo – you know, you get a photo of me with longer legs, a rounder chin, a thinner waist ... he'll have computer software that will make me perfect for you."

"Oh Charlotte, really, you are perfect for us already," replied Peter, though he had probably never seen a magazine or online photo that had not been retouched to correct nature's failure to make every woman perfect.

Next came the filmed advert. Charlotte would walk through the carpet showroom in her 'signature' leather trousers, stop and put a leg up on a roll of carpet and say, "When I'm in the Swansea Bay area, I love to shop at Harrison Carpets. You'll be amazed at the prices in this year's sales. Come in and see us now – that's Harrison Carpets, Abbey Industrial Estate, Neath."

She did three takes and in each she tried to sound just that little bit excited about carpets. Peter applauded each one enthusiastically. The photographer - now turned director – did at least thank her at the end of the third one.

Charlotte shook hands, thanked people and even signed a couple of autographs for the lads in the warehouse. They looked pleased to meet a fairly famous person and she was shown in to their break room while they found things for her to sign. She allowed herself a wry smile at the calendar of pictures of scantily-clad women, clearly this was not a workplace that had female employees or thoughts about equality. Was she any better posing with a leg up on a roll of carpet though?

She would have pondered that question for far longer had her eye not been caught by a newspaper lying on one of the chairs. It was quite rare to see a paper format for a newspaper these days, but they were still passed around in workplaces. Open on the chair was the gossip page and staring back at her from it was a photo of herself at three in the morning, looking rough, dishevelled and embarrassed. For a moment she was impressed that in less than twelve hours a photo could go from outside Danny's house to a break room in Neath. It was almost as though the story had been written in advance.

That was hardly the point, though. 'Late Night Shame of TV's Charlotte!' screamed the headline while the opening paragraph speculated in excited terms what it could mean that the 'leggy Channel 6 lovely' was leaving her co-presenter's house late at night. She leaned forward to discover more about what she had done but a hand closed the paper rapidly.

The hand belonged to Derek, the warehouse manager, who had been searching around for a sports magazine for her to sign before he noticed what she was reading.

"Sorry about that, luv, no-one's business but your own."

"And the people who read it," she observed.

"No, well, no, I mean ..." he stammered awkwardly, wanting to deny reading it but knowing that she knew that he had read it excitedly only earlier that day, "... I mean he's a very lucky man if it's true."

"I'd say he is a lucky man indeed," she agreed, thinking of Danny and Ed sharing a bottle of wine and some laughter in their apartment, "but perhaps this is one I won't sign, if that's okay?"

*   *   *   *   *

Charlotte stood outside Orchard House in the centre of Swansea. It was a rather innocuous office building that had seen a lot of better days. She had stepped into the toilets at Swansea station to change into something less conspicuous and she had tied as much of her dyed blonde hair under a beanie hat as she could manage. Hopefully she was no longer a reasonably famous sports presenter, more just an ordinary Welsh citizen. She pressed the intercom button for 'Room 8'.

"Hi, it's ... a ... I think that you're expecting me," she garbled, "Danny said ... Danny told you to expect me after I had been to the carpet place."

"Ah yes," said the voice at the other end of the intercom, "press 1, 3, 7 and 9 and the door should open. Then come up to the first floor and turn right."

Charlotte swore under her breath, what was this, some kind of maze? She entered the code and went into the building. The entry way was draughty and the paint was peeling from the walls. This 'third sector' did not have much money, whoever they were.

Nervously she stepped up the staircase and then along the corridor to Room 8. In there was a chaos that she was not expecting.

Charlotte was to describe it many years later as a madhouse. The furniture and computers had all been piled in a corner, five or six staff members were rushing around trying to work out what to do, while a middle-aged man in overalls was attempting to lift the carpet up. It was this man who spoke to her.

"Hi," he said, dropping the carpet to offer an outstretched hand to shake, "I'm Ceri. I'm the Manager."

Ah, thought Charlotte, back in a land where 'Ceri' was a man's name. She shook him by the hand.

"Pleased to meet you, Ceri ...?"

"Oh no, don't worry about that, it's the voluntary sector, we're all on first name terms here."

"In that case, I'm Charlotte."

"I know who you are."

It was a statement empty of intent or threat but it still took Charlotte aback somewhat. This did not seem to deter Ceri the Manager, who had started signalling to his staff to roll the carpet up the other way.

"Sorry about this, we decided that we needed new carpet, but none of us are really qualified in this field."

"Don't you have a plan?"

"How do you mean?"

"You know, like an action plan or a to do list or an order of business."

"Yes, yes," said Ceri busily and brought out a crumpled piece of paper from the pocket of his weathered jacket. Charlotte could see that halfway down it was written 'remove old carpet'.

"Who is the administrator here?"

There was laughter from the people in the room and Charlotte felt slightly offended, as if her naïvety was being mocked. She expected that in London, not in Swansea.

"'Scuse them," explained Ceri, "we haven't had admin in years. Never can afford it – everyone types their own e-mails in this sector."

"How do you get things organised then?"

"As you can see ..." said Ceri with a pride that Charlotte thought was altogether misplaced.

In fact, the more Charlotte watched the shambles of a scene before her, the more she realised that she was in a place to help. She had only just met these people, but she intended to show that she was more than just a television presenter who had stepped in from the wrong street.

"Hey, you!" she said rather inelegantly to a tall man in an orange hoodie who was struggling to pull up the carpet from the corner of the room, "How big do you think this room is – feet by feet?"

"Ricky," he replied to identify himself, "I'd say eight by nine."

"Thank you," said Charlotte and started to fiddle with her phone. It only took a quick search for a number before she was listening to a ringing tone. Ricky stood and watched her.

"Harrison Carpets – the best deals on carpets in Neath and the Swansea Bay area. How may I direct your call this morning?" said a woman who had clearly passed her GCSE Customer Services module.

"I need to speak to Peter."

"Oh, I'm sorry, he's in a meeting right now, if you would leave your name and message I will pass those details on to him."

Ah, thought Charlotte, that would be part two of the module, always blocking calls to senior staff while sounding reasonable. She had got an 'A' in that.

"Tell him that Charlotte is on the phone and needs to talk to him about this morning's photos. Then he'll come to the phone."

"I'm sorry Miss, he is in a meeting right now, but if I take a message ..."

"I tell you what," said Charlotte, interrupting someone who had only got a 'C' in her blocking calls to senior staff module, "you tell him what I have just said and if he is still in a meeting then I will do as you say."

There was a pause while the customer services assistant at the other end of the phone pondered her options. Charlotte was relying on fear and job insecurity to push the belief that the call was urgent.

Just as she was starting to lose confidence, there was a clicking sound, a change of line and then the oleaginous tones of Peter the Carpet Man were greeting her enthusiastically. Who said that they taught you nothing useful in school?

"Hi Peter, no it's not about the photos really. I need to order a carpet. Note this down – eight by nine feet, your best hard-wearing office carpet, light grey. Get your fitter to park his van outside the NCP car park on

91

Orchard Street, Swansea and a man named Ricky will show him where to lay it – he'll be wearing an orange hoodie, he's tall and he's got a black goatee beard."

"Of course, we have just the thing in stock."

"Top quality – if it costs then take it out of my fee."

"Cost? Oh no, of course not. Anything we can do for our local celebrity. You are our face of carpet, you only need to ask."

"Thank you, Peter. You're very kind."

Ceri looked slightly impressed and Ricky shook Charlotte's hand as a proper introduction. At last her moderate amount of fame had helped someone. She liked that thought.

"Come down to Room 13, it's also one of ours. There's a kettle there, though it'll have to be soya milk, we don't have dairy."

Charlotte followed Ceri along a narrow corridor to another small room. This had better carpet but she did think for a minute about whether she should have ordered two rolls. This room was full of papers lying around on tables, folders, files and paperwork of the kind that she seemed to remember was supposed to disappear years ago with 'the paperless office'.

Ceri flicked a switch on a kettle sitting in the corner.

"Channel 6's top sports presenter in our little old office, eh? There's one. What brings you here?"

"Danny said there's something called ... 'the third sector'."

Charlotte almost expected Ceri to hush her and indicate that they had to talk in code and keep the right side of a large blocking transmitter of some kind.

She took out the card that simply read '8 Orchard'. This seemed to be her passport into this new world and Ceri started to explain a little background.

The organisation was called 'Swansea Volunteer Bureau' and it operated at almost no cost through volunteers and helpers. Ceri was paid, though nothing on the scale of a London wage, and part of his job was trying to find money to keep the operation going. At first Charlotte assumed that this might mean robbing banks or defrauding businesses, but it turned out that there were people, companies and organisations who would be prepared to give money to help them. Charlotte asked what they received in return. Ceri's answer of 'satisfaction, a feeling of having helped, giving back to the community' made no sense in a world where everyone learned in school that money is the root of all happiness.

However, what silenced Charlotte was when Ceri described an alternative world. It was a world in which people did not have to pay for school fees and there were organisations called 'charities' who could help those who did not have enough food or clothes or who had nowhere to live. There were no hospital bills! In this other world, hospitals treated people for free – everyone contributed a bit into their budget so that they knew that the hospital was there for them if they were ever ill.

Ceri talked about a wonderful volunteering project in north-east Wales where volunteers sat in hospital operating rooms and talked to people while they were being operated on. It was such a strange and simple idea and yet survival rates had increased as a result. Ricky, who she had met earlier, was something called a 'youth worker', someone who provided activities for young people to help them grow and develop and cope with the adult world. It was as if Charlotte's world had been covered in deep snow for twenty-three years and only now was the snow melting and she was seeing what was really there.

"It's impossible," was her conclusion.

"It's not," replied Ceri, "that's the third sector - or voluntary sector if you prefer that title. We know that if you can get people past the idea that only money matters, you will be amazed how good people feel when they give something back."

Charlotte shook her head and sipped at her tea quietly. She was so used to coffee-free coffee in Channel 6 that she was finding even third sector tea strong and a little unsettling. She asked Ceri how he had become involved.

"I grew up in these parts but I got a job in Ipswich and spent some time there. Moved about quite a bit with a group of friends – we never really had money, but it was fun. You probably don't think that I sound local."

Charlotte thought her ability to judge accents was the least interesting part of this conversation, "I've never heard of moving about before. You go to school, you leave and get a job. Anyway, how do you know Danny?"

"I met Danny when I was working for the LGBT Centre of Excellence. Really impressed how far he has gone working that 'bloke about town' charm. Good cover story being in a relationship by the way, although I noticed that it's not him in the 'papers. Always the same when the world goes conservative, it gets frightened and clings to 'tradition', men always get it easier."

Charlotte idly sorted through some papers lying on the table next to her, "No-one's doing your administration, you say?"

"We all muck in, really. It does mean that there is a backlog of paperwork."

Charlotte sighed and looked around her at all the unsorted filing and folders. However impressed she was by Ceri's commitment to helping others, his administration was shocking.

"I'd like to think about helping you out. I don't mean carpet, that was a lucky coincidence, I mean finding a way to help. One thing though – Danny said that it was dangerous, why aren't you worried about being shut down or arrested or something?"

Ceri laughed and pointed out of the window towards Swansea city centre.

"It's Swansea. I still wouldn't risk having this conversation outside the building but all the same, we are in a run-down office block in Swansea. Yes, we are probably being spied on and our volunteers have to operate carefully and in secret, but no-one in government is expecting the revolution to start in Orchard House. At least, that's what we hope. A couple of years ago we broke the CCTV camera out there and it wasn't repaired. The revolution won't be televised."

Charlotte looked at the folders around her and muttered, "the revolution won't be televised, but it will need an efficient filing system."

* * * * *

"Hi Mam!" shouted Charlotte as she opened the door to the family home.

She threw her suitcase to one side in the front room and nodded at her sister, who was slumped on the sofa eating crisps.

"Hi Heather," she said and heard a guitar chord in her head.

"Hi Charlotte," was the sulky reply, accompanied by a similar sound.

Visiting your parents brings out something of the teenager in everyone. Charlotte left her suitcase in the way of anyone moving around the front room and walked into the kitchen to greet her mother.

"Charlotte darling, you've grown!"

"No, I haven't Mam, I just dress differently now."

In honesty, Charlotte thought her mother had shrunk slightly, a costly foot operation added to the list of ailments affecting her and paid for by her fairly famous daughter. They hugged warmly.

"Well, I'm going to cook for everyone, there are things that I can still do. It's great to have you home."

"Is Dad coming around?"

"Not this time. It's different with you two being older."

"I see that she is still living with you. Isn't it time she and Jon moved out?"

"I can hear you!" called Heather from the front room.

"I know, that's why I'm being rude about you!" shouted back her sister.

"Jon's a lovely boy, he's no trouble. Move out? Do you remember how expensive housing is? What's the average age for leaving home now – thirty, I think? You're an exception."

"I suppose I am."

"Of course, you've got a man of your own now, I hear."

"Yeah, tell us about it 'Sex Shame Charlotte'!" yelled the voice from the front room.

"I haven't you know, it's not what you think. And I'm not ashamed, there's nothing to be ashamed about!"

"You're quite right," said her Mam, manoeuvring awkwardly around the oven, "don't be ashamed of what you've done."

Charlotte shook her head and walked back into the front room to confront her critic. Before she could speak, her eye caught something on the mantelpiece, alongside the family photos, the flowers and the shells found on the beach. It was her. She moved over to look at the photo frame carefully.

"Oy! Sis! I'm trying to watch telly here, get out the way!"

Heather did look older than Charlotte remembered. Her blonde hair was now short and she was looking heavier than before. Slumping in a baggy jumper was not exactly showing her best features, mind you. Charlotte turned her attention back to herself.

It was a framed publicity shot. She could remember the day it was taken – long, blonde hair blown by a fan, staggering to a convenient point in crazily high boots, then being directed how to stand and to bend forward. There was that winning smile amid the make-up creation of Tamsin and Sarah and then signed across the bottom of the photo was : "From Charlotte With Love", three kisses and three hearts. She smiled

97

at herself, not bad for a girl from Aberystwyth Crescent, Barry.

"Yeah, yeah, yeah, you're the famous daughter, we get it," muttered Heather, "don't think I care. You won't get me bragging down the supermarket about my famous sister or anything."

Heather was lying. She had made a steady income selling publicity photos to people at work with fake signatures that she had added. She had become quite good at being the fake Charlotte, the three hearts under the name being a touch that she was particularly proud about. However, she was not in a mood to be part of her sister's glorious homecoming and so she stood up and made loud footfalls on the stairs as she headed for her bedroom.

Charlotte watched her leave and stood in the middle of the front room with a blank expression.

"You're going to have to apologise to your sister," said her mother from the kitchen.

"Mam!" shouted Charlotte, "That's not fair!"

Being around your parents brings out the teenager in everyone.

*   *   *   *   *

Charlotte did climb the stairs though and looked in on her old bedroom with a certain nostalgia. It still had many of her things there, but now her sister had moved an exercise bike in there and her mother had spread out bills across the bedside table. Charlotte made a note that she needed to organise those. Firstly, there was her sister to deal with.

She knocked on Heather's door and when she heard 'go away!' she went in.

Heather's room had changed quite a lot in the last few years, it seemed. The teenage posters and flyers for music festivals out of Heather's reach had gone, the bed now had a pull-out section for when Jon was staying and the walls had been painted a more sober green. Heather was curled in a sulky ball in the corner of the bed.

"I'm sorry sis," started Charlotte, sitting down next to her on the bed, "I need to talk to you properly anyway. You were sitting there where I used to sit with Dad commenting about the football."

"And now you do it for real – big whoop."

"No, I don't. You watch carefully, I'm not allowed to ask anything but superficial questions. But it could be different, I have met people who want something different. It's incredible and it could change everything – for me, for Mam, for you ..."

Heather looked at her with a mixture of fear and puzzlement on her face. Charlotte suddenly thought that she looked older then twenty-one.

"I'm pregnant," announced Heather with a waterfall of tears following.

"What? How did that happen?"

"You need me to tell you?"

"No, I mean ... are you sure?"

"Of course, I'm bloody sure! I stole three pregnancy tests from the supermarket and they were all positive."

"Oh, okay well, I mean, is it Jon's?"

"Is 'Sex Shame Charlotte' calling me a bit of a slut? You should see how many men the papers link you with!"

"It's all nonsense and Danny is gay anyway ..."

"You really know how to pick 'em, sis," said Heather, before crying again.

Charlotte sat and stared at her sister. She was simultaneously thrilled at the idea of being an aunt but also unsure what to do about her sister's distress. She tried to put an arm on her shoulder as an awkward sisterly gesture of solidarity. Heather's words came in a tumble between tears.

"We can't afford it. Mam can't afford a baby in here. You know what will happen – soon as they know I'm pregnant, they'll sack me. You know it happens all the time. Jon can't support me, who'll do the childcare? Mam's exhausted enough already ..."

The words came in a flood that washed away Charlotte's happy thoughts about becoming an aunt.

"You're not thinking of ... you know ... getting a procedure to stop it?"

"How the hell would we afford that operation, then? I'm not going to some backstreet place and get messed up by one of those unofficial doctors."

"I'd help – you know I would, I've been sending money to Mam and didn't you get those jewellery shop vouchers?"

"Yes, but you know it won't be enough and we can't live off your boobs forever."

"We'll think of something ..."

"No, we won't. We won't. There is nothing, nothing you can say to make this better. I just don't want ... I just don't want anything. How did I get into this mess?"

Charlotte watched her sister cry and then simply said, "Fuck."

"Yes, I know, I did listen in Biology lessons."

Heather had never heard her sister swear before and it seemed to make their conversation swerve off its normal road. Charlotte was shaking her head vigorously.

"That's not what I mean. I said that because it has occurred to me for the first time that you are the adult here. All my bloody life I've thought that I was the adult in this family and you were some whining, preening teen princess but suddenly ... suddenly, I am the one off gallivanting while you are holding it all together. I don't know why I didn't see it before."

"You were too busy having the latest pedicure treatment."

Charlotte smiled weakly at her sister and then leant over and patted her stomach, something that Heather would have to become used to from total strangers over the coming months.

"This is what's not right though - little Heathcliffe of Heatherina in there, my little niece or nephew, why should she have the same life that Mam had, that we have had? Why?"

"You know how the saying goes, love can't buy you happiness, only money can."

"Generation after generation doing shit jobs, being replaced by computers, internet shopping closing down all the shops, everyone has qualifications but none of them mean anything. Posh schools for the children in

101

Surrey, McDonald's for the children in Barry, nothing but money. Money, money, money. Nothing else matters and all we do is repeat the same damn mistakes family after family, generation after generation. I want something different for Heather Mark 2!"

"We're not calling her 'Mark'."

"Shut up. There's a group of people - volunteers they are called ..."

"I know about volunteering, I was made to do it by the Job Centre Plus Website when I was out of work. Dare say I'll be logging online to register as unemployed again soon as the bump shows."

Charlotte stood up and started pacing her sister's bedroom. Heather stared at her until her head became dizzy.

"They need organising though. No administrators! It's crazy, they're the most important people. We could change this country. Heather - one day they will raise statues to your unborn child in thanks for this moment!"

"You're talking some weird ..."

The sound of their mother's voice calling for them silenced any further discussion. Heather simply touched her belly and put a finger to her lips. Charlotte nodded. Mam would be thrilled to think of becoming a grandmother, but the money worries would be bad for her health. It would be up to them both to parent her now.

* * * * *

Charlotte spent two more days with her family before heading back to London. Back in work, she laughed and joked with Tamsin and Sarah, both of whom tried to subtly and not so subtly find out what had changed between her and Danny. They had an apprentice with them now – Michelle – who busied herself running around after them, making coffee-free coffee and desperately trying to learn everything.

Sarah explained to Michelle that Charlotte's skin may have suffered from several days in the rain and cold of Wales, especially as they had heard that there were no proper moisturising creams there. Michelle nodded. It was the perfect opportunity for Charlotte to ask casually if she could have some time alone with Danny when he arrived. There were suppressed giggles all around and knowing winks and nods.

Danny arrived an hour before recording as usual, asking only for some gel for his hair, a slight trim for his beard and perhaps a new waistcoat from the collection. Charlotte grabbed him by the arm and pulled him into a backroom. She was conscious that there were probably one, two or three pairs of ears pressed to the door for gossip.

"I met those people," said Charlotte.

"Who?"

"The carpet people."

"Good, good," said Danny before realising too late that this was a symbolic conversation, "Ah, did you go to the orchard, you mean?"

"For crying out loud you're bad at this! Yes, we need to pick some bloody apples, that's what I mean."

"Yes, apples. Good."

Charlotte stared at him. Did no-one else have the skills for this?

"I need you to square it with the Channel - with Ladislau - that I am going to work at weekends in London but go back to Wales during the week. My mother's ill, my sister's having a tough time, I need some time to be around them, tell them that kind of thing. I'll still go to the gym and do personal appearances, but they should be scheduled around the weekend. Do you understand?"

"Yes," said Danny, trying to follow Charlotte's gaze to the keyhole of the door and then dropping his voice to a whisper, "we've got several weeks of stories about you as cover. We'll be having a public fight in a few weeks, then there will be speculation that you're pregnant, the next week that you are unhealthily thin and ..."

"Fat one week, thin the next?"

"Oh, no-one keeps track of these things. One of us will have to have a fling while we're apart. Don't worry, we'll keep the story going this end. And yes to asking Ladislau - our ratings shot up after you dominated the gossip columns, advertisers love you, the Channel will do anything for you right now."

"Good, then kiss me!"

"Ugh, no!"

"You still know how to flatter a girl."

Danny did not have time to consider a clever response as Charlotte was rubbing her lips across his, not open, just back and forth. He pushed her off and wiped his lips with a hand.

"Smeared lipstick - just in case anyone listening at the door sells the story to the papers," Charlotte explained.

"You're getting good at this!" muttered Danny as Charlotte threw open the door of the backroom to see three pairs of heels quickly dispersing as their owners pretended to have been doing something very important near to the door.

*   *   *   *   *

Charlotte's first task in Swansea was to organise files and folders. Paper was the safest way to communicate. Messages by phone or computer were insecure and everyone knew that storing things in 'the cloud' was encouraged by companies so that they could search through the data for anything interesting. The humble folder with sheets of paper, divided by coloured card, was the first tool of protest.

Room 13 became her admin room. Each shelf held folders concerning different areas of volunteering, their operations and their funding. That was just for Swansea. Tip-offs came in of people in other cities running similar schemes and she talked to them. 'Who is your Administrator?' she would ask, knowing that anyone who claimed to have one was probably a government or company spy.

Back in London, she encouraged Ed to start a wine-tasting club. The model was simple - claim to be charging for the event and then when people tried to pay, explain that it was free. Then explain the whole concept of volunteering. If people still wanted to pay, they could make a donation to a third sector organisation. This way funding increased too.

Each person who took away the message of volunteering was encouraged to set up their own project - Charlotte's folders were running out of shelf space. It was then that she hit on an idea that truly revolutionised the movement. She called the University.

So many young people went straight into jobs at sixteen now that universities were not what they once were, but even the minority of students who engaged in higher study had time on their hands. At first it was internal - 'want to meet girls /boys? Try Spanish study club!' ran one poster - but then she started to find that students wanted to do more and that there was a place for them in all the organisations who they were supporting. The word went out around British University campuses and suddenly 'the Swansea thing' was being talked about in hushed tones out of the way of lecturers and corridor cameras.

Anthea arrived seven months later, just as Charlotte was despairing of the size of the task. She came from one of the wealthier families on the Gower peninsula but had heard about volunteering through a friend of a friend at University. She had no wish to jump into a gorge, visit an old person, deliver blood supplies by motorbike or any of the other opportunities that Swansea Volunteer Bureau could offer. She took one look at Room 13 and knew what she could do.

"I'm here to help with the admin," she declared brightly.

"What? No-one says that!"

"I've heard," said Anthea breezily, throwing her work bag over one of the desks, "that you are working all hours that you are here. You can't do it all on your own. Me, junior admin."

Charlotte laughed and gave Anthea an unexpected hug.

"Woah, okay," laughed Anthea, "Look, I've seen what's going on at the university, are you in touch with other Unis?"

"And colleges," replied Charlotte, indicating a shelf of folders on a far wall, "pretty much set up in all of them now."

"All of the UK?"

"No idea."

"That's my next job then. We need to make this a British movement, even a European movement. A youth movement - imagine if people from Swansea could, say, go to Stuttgart. Just spend time in each other's countries, find out what things are like. They'd come back and improve things here."

"That could never happen."

"Like you went to London and changed things in Barry."

Suddenly Charlotte was suspicious.

"Flattery, eh? How come you know so much about me?"

"I have a friend who is pregnant. She came across a mothers-to-be club that was meeting on the quiet a few months ago. Heather was one of the guest speakers."

"Heather who?" asked Charlotte, trying to think of famous pregnant women named Heather.

"Your sister Heather."

"Now I know you're lying."

"She said that you would say that."

"Did she now?"

"Yes," said Anthea, seeing that Charlotte was intrigued, "she said to call you by your codename."

"My codename?"

"Yes, Loser With A Capital L."

"I'm going to kill her," said Charlotte with affection.

Anthea's story seemed to be confirmed by a few discreet phone calls and she started to busy herself with sorting out folders. Ricky the Youth Worker appeared with a drill. The volunteering revolution was going to need more shelf space.

*   *   *   *   *

People became careless though. It was inevitable across such a large operation and it caused immediate problems. Sometimes it was personality battles within groups, sometimes it was founders not wanting to lose control of their projects, sometimes it was just careless advertising that alerted the authorities to the organisation and sometimes - too often for Charlotte's liking - it was a lack of organisation within an organisation.

In London, two of the UK's top police officers were handed the task of trying to uncover and stop 'the third sector' before it spread too far. Randall and Korda worked for the UK Enforcement Agency, a crime investigation team set up by a Prime Minister who had watched too many American police dramas and wanted to set up the UK's own FBI. Just as Charlotte operated her network as subtlely as she could do from Room 13 in Swansea, Randall and Korda set up their own room in the back of West Hillingdon police station in London. They were determined to find the mastermind behind this operation.

They were helped when the Prime Minister announced to the Conservative Party Conference that there would be a new crime added to the statute book. Needing to be seen as dynamic and commanding, the PM explained that the greatest economist that Britain had ever produced had once said that 'you can't buck the market' and therefore it would be made a crime to try to buck the market. The recent outbreak of 'volunteering' (and not true volunteering such as that ordered by the Job Centre website) was undermining British business. To a rising crescendo of cheering and applause, the Prime Minister declared that 'so-called volunteers are taking - no, stealing – British jobs from British workers. Every time you see someone working for free, they are stopping a British worker being paid for a British job!'

Randall and Korda received reports of volunteering from all over the country but they noticed a pattern in several of them - a wine-tasting club in London where a man named Ed with a connection to Channel 6 sports programming was outed as a volunteer in a dispute about pinot grigio, an employee in a carpet company in Neath who claimed to have worked for free as a favour to a Channel 6 sports presenter and a tip-off from a teenager in Swansea about a man named Ricky who ran a gorge walking trip for a youth club in South Wales. Was there a connection with Wales and a connection with Channel 6 sport? An 'invitation' was sent out to Charlotte to attend an interview at West Hillingdon police station. Their mistake was to give her fair warning.

Charlotte knew that she had to give the performance of her life. Her time as a sports reporter had taught her how to perform but she knew that she needed expert help. Tamsin was only too happy to do an 'unofficial' job.

"You've gone for red streaks, then?" said Charlotte when she saw her in the make-up room at the Channel.

"Gotta keep it fresh. What are you going for?" asked Tamsin as she removed her ever-present shades and sorted through her make-up bags.

"I've got an interview later but I don't want it to be business. I want to look like it's a night out, big heels especially, but not over the top."

"We can do that no problem, girl. Interview though? Not leaving us, I hope?"

"Oh no, just a side project, if you like."

"Phew, you've been the best we've had, there's more to you than the others," said Tamsin, running her hands through Charlotte's hair, pondering styling, "just remember that an interview is like a performance. Sell them something, like you do on telly every Saturday. Give them a blank space and let them fill in the story."

Charlotte nodded and sat back in the chair, "Oh and I'll need a taxi to take me to West Hillingdon when we're done, I need heels that I can't walk in."

* * * * *

The taxi dropped Charlotte off outside the police station in West Hillingdon. It was out west in London but Charlotte was not fooled into thinking that this was any remote police force that she would be seeing. She staggered into the station on the improbable heels that Tamsin had chosen. She was stylish but suggestive and with all those little touches - false eyelashes, false nails - that would make her look like her main concern was fashion, not politics.

The desk sergeant was a little taken aback when she walked in and Charlotte could not resist offering him an autograph. He called some of the other officers into reception and they would have posed for photos had not a tall man in a dark suit arrived. This was Randall.

Charlotte gave a wave and blew a kiss to her new fans in reception and followed Randall through to a back room. In it was a table and three chairs, one of which was occupied by a middle-aged woman in a sombre suit. This was Korda. Charlotte's nerves were calmed when she saw a camera in the middle of the table pointing to where she would sit. It was just a television performance, after all.

There was no formal introduction, just the locking of the door and the indication for Charlotte to sit down in the chair opposite the camera. Korda looked at her suspiciously.

"You understand that you are here for very serious reasons?" she said.

"Oh yes," said Charlotte, before pausing for just long enough to add, "why exactly am I here?"

"You know," said Korda.

Charlotte surveyed them carefully. As an interviewer she had become skilled in looking at the clues that people gave. Randall was wearing a wedding ring she noted, this would be useful. People always underestimated the prejudice of the married man, especially if he is attracted to a young woman. Korda was clearly in charge though. How would a woman wearing no make up and with a hairstyle that was simply slicked back take to an over made-up woman from Channel 6, she wondered?

"Things going well with your boyfriend?" asked Randall.

Charlotte needed to work out what they knew and until that was decided, she would play dumb. She had made a career of it.

"Oh, it's great. I'm so lucky to have found him," she replied, giving Randall a sly wink.

"You close?" he asked.

"Well, you know what the papers say but, yes, what a journey - me, a girl from Wales to get here and ... wow!"

"You've certainly come far," commented Korda, "but whether you have left home behind is another matter. You're saying that you and Danny are a very close couple, then?"

Charlotte smiled and nodded.

"Do you know he's gay?" asked Randall matter-of-factly.

"No! He never told me!" said Charlotte, not very convincingly.

Korda shook her head and slid a black and white picture of Ed across the table to her.

"This man has been spotted around his apartment," she said, "and he is implicated in one of these so-called 'volunteering' activities that is damaging this country."

Okay, so they had Danny's file and they had staked out his apartment. She doubted that they had done this to her yet, but she needed to be careful. It was time to give them a little of what they wanted to know.

"Look, you know he is gay. You must also know that that could ruin him if it ever got out. So, I hang out with a gay guy, he's sweet and lovely. What's your problem with that?"

"We think that this Danny has contacts that could be dangerous. What do you know about them?" asked Korda.

Ah, thought Charlotte, so she was not being accused directly. She looked at them and thought about what to say, while trying to give the impression of a woman with no original thought in her head. Again, Channel 6 expected this of her every week.

Randall interrupted her apparent lack of thought, "You know that we can torture you, right? We are not one of these third world countries that have outlawed torture, we could beat it out of you."

"But I'm taping an advert tomorrow!" lied Charlotte, reminding them that if she did disappear or appear with new injuries, people would notice.

Korda pushed her chair back dramatically in a move that Charlotte thought had been copied from bad American TV dramas and then leaned over the table at her.

"You don't fool me Missy, you know what's going on and if you don't start talking we're going to have real trouble with you!"

"I don't know what you mean," replied Charlotte, maintaining her innocence.

This now would be the performance of a lifetime. She needed to give them something which sounded like a confession and which was also believable.

"Okay, I'll level with you," she said, then turning to look at Randall, "You're a man of the world."

Charlotte aimed a wink at him and, sure enough, he was starting to look a little bit disgusted with her. Good, disgusted was just the emotion she needed to make this believable.

"Yeah, Danny's gay and yes I know that and have always known that. He's a great cover for me though. Can you imagine how often I get hit on when I look this good?"

She wiggled as she spoke these last lines and watched Randall fight back a smile that he did not want to admit to making.

"I look hot. When I dance, men fall around me. I need the cover of saying, 'oy back off, I've got a boyfriend, you read the papers'. It works. What happens when I want a bit of ... well, you know a girl gets lonely in the city here ... I can pick and choose. None of them will ever go to the papers either because the papers are so convinced that Danny and I are about to announce the wedding of the century."

She pouted a little at Randall and gave him a look that hopefully said, 'wouldn't you?' His face said disgust. It was too easy. Korda was staring at this performance only looking half-convinced.

"So you're saying that you use him as a cover for getting a shag every now and then?" asked Korda.

"He gets to spend time with his boyfriend. Who are we harming?"

The two interrogators looked at each other, not completely convinced but also starting to believe. Charlotte thought that she could read expressions. That is, she could read expressions on faces that had not had botox treatment. There was absolutely no botox to be found in the UK Enforcement Agency.

"I did say we could torture you if we needed to," repeated Korda.

"How attached are you to your fingernails?" asked Randall in a voice that was supposed to be intimidating.

"Not very - I put these red ones on this morning but I don't think that they really work with the outfit, you know? Could I have a set of nails in black, do you think?"

Korda kicked her chair over in frustration. People were normally intimidated by this point. However, the silence brought an odd decision.

"Let's leave her," said Randall and the two unexpectedly left the room, leaving Charlotte locked in.

For a moment, she sat there and wondered what was going on. Then she picked up her bag and thought how stupid of them to leave her with her phone. It was halfway to her hand before she realised that of course, that was the point! She was being watched and any call that she made would be monitored. They wanted her to call Danny and tell him to watch out or to prepare for a raid. Instead, she loaded up the old fruit-matching game that she had played while talking to Sadie years ago. She just had to concentrate on looking like she was not thinking, while all the time thinking of how she was going to get out of the situation.

When Korda and Randall's team of technical experts had spent an hour watching Charlotte match strawberries, apples and pears to gain access to a bonus level, they gave up on that technique. The interrogators returned to the room and once again Korda's face was red with manufactured anger. Charlotte motioned for her to wait until she had finished the bonus screen. That brought genuine anger.

"Do you know the trouble you are in? Do you even understand?"

Charlotte calmly folded away her phone and looked at them both directly.

"You two are intelligent, I know this. You want the truth. I've told you a bit of it but you want it all, don't you?"

The two interrogators sat down on their chairs and listened intently.

"Yes, I use my relationship with Danny to cover having sex. It's what I do, but I work bloody hard. You know my sister has a baby - check when I last did promo appearances for baby supply shops. How much do you think I got from them in baby items? I did a product launch for the supermarket where she works just before she told them that she was pregnant - they found it harder to sack her once they knew. Yes, I once got a roll of damn carpet ... and a host of other things from everyone who I have exploited because I am famous. Because I am not completely an airhead bimbo, I know that one day there will be someone younger and prettier with better-shaped boobs than me and then what will I be? I'm guilty, then. Guilty of milking the bloody system for everything I can get, but don't you tell me that I did anything for free. Free! I worked my arse off for every promotional gift. That bloody carpet? Do you know what an oily git that man from Harrison's Carpets is? Call me a thief yes, but don't you dare call me someone who does anything for nothing!"

The two interrogators stared at her. It was a confession, but of a crime that was nothing like the one that they were investigating. She was a money-grabbing, gold-digging airhead bimbo but that was completely the opposite of the volunteers who they were looking for. Both of them were startled and unsure of what to do.

Eventually, Korda sighed and said, "You can go."

Charlotte thanked them and smiled. When she reached reception she flirted with the men at the desk as she waited for her taxi. She knew that she would be followed, monitored and trailed for days but she was leaving after a convincing story.

Korda and Randall watched Charlotte's progress across to the taxi from a window.

"Still say she's an airhead bimbo who got lucky with more looks than talent," said Randall.

"Now, now officer, didn't you do the course on not judging suspects?" rebuked Korda, "She's a conniving, clever bitch that one, but she is gaming the system not trying to end it."

They say that in those parts of the police force where they never quite accepted the revolution that Charlotte would administer, they still have a photo of her leaving the police station taken from the CCTV film taken that day. It is to remind them that sometimes the administrative genius behind the revolutionary movement is someone wearing stripper heels.

*   *   *   *   *

Charlotte returned home to Barry knowing that she would be followed, monitored and variously recorded until they decided that she was probably harmless. She had delegated much of the work in Swansea to Anthea and she trusted her to be filing efficiently. However, the days of flinging her bag messily around the front room on arrival had gone. Now she brought her family together for an urgent, whispered conference.

"We have to act as if someone is listening to everything we say and do in here," she whispered.

"We've been living in a terraced house for twenty years, we already do," dead-panned her mother.

"Really?" asked Heather with a touch of shock, "You mean everything I've done in my room has been heard? What even ..."

They never found out quite what Heather considered her noisiest or most extreme act as at that moment baby Jolene started crying, an event amplified through the baby monitor in the front room. Heather rolled her tired eyes and nodded to the other two as if there were a choice as to who would sort this out.

"That's brilliant!" described Charlotte.

"You wait till you're a mother, then," grumbled Heather.

"No, this is brilliant – when we need to discuss anything that doesn't need to be overheard, we wait until Jolene is crying. She's our best and brightest revolutionary recruit!"

"Viva la revolution!" muttered Heather sarcastically.

A week later Korda and Randall had the tech team's report on Charlotte's home - a week of horrible, screaming baby noises that no-one wanted to listen through and the phone messages were all from

118

Charlotte's sister saying things like, 'So soz Anth, no party this week, laters, Hxx'. The tech team were begging to be allowed to return to London.

*   *   *   *   *

Most of you will know how this story ends as it is well-covered in history books. However, the spread of 'the third sector' really took hold once people realised that it worked.

As an example, Charlotte sneaked out from a mid-week FA Cup fixture between Leeds United and Sheffield Wednesday to visit Leeds Volunteer Bureau. Like most of them, it was in a run-down office building on the edge of a city centre, but it had started the work of promoting volunteering and matching potential volunteers to opportunities. Anthea had been in contact to help them gain some energetic students and Charlotte found an office with a buzz of enthusiasm. She met the admin student and had a flick through the files - she made a few comments about listing names alphabetically by surname rather than first name, but generally they were in good admin shape.

She was introduced to Terry and Judie, a couple with small children who had come in to the Bureau to find out more about the movement. Their children were now going to volunteer-run football and dancing classes on a Tuesday night and the couple had been shocked to find that they had an evening to themselves.

"Gives you chance to spend some quality time together, eh?" said Charlotte with a wink.

"We slump on the sofa and just thank God to have a moment to breathe, to be honest," said Terry.

"I have a nice, chilled glass of wine," said Judie.

"Or two," added Terry.

Then Judie gave Charlotte a big hug and thanked her profusely.

"They say that you're the one who invented volunteering," she said.

"Not really," said Charlotte, "but if you really want to thank me then start a group of your own or help out with a local group."

"Oh, we haven't really got any skills to offer," said Terry apologetically.

"What do you like doing?"

"I don't know. I follow the football - love your show - I do a bit of DIY ..."

"I go for a run every now and then ..." added Judie.

Charlotte shrugged, "That would be sports team coaching or an intergenerational project bringing young people together with older people who need DIY jobs done and you Judie should be using social media to start a local running club. Routes, times, training - start online and see how many people are looking for that kind of thing."

Judie gave Charlotte another hug and thanked her again. Terry coughed nervously.

"Thanks, but I can't stay long - Terry, would you do me a favour? There's a red car out there, a Nissan Quinoa or something which has followed me here from London."

"I see it, want me to block it in or knock the headlights out or something?"

"No, I want you to help me sell a story. We'll go down to the corner there and have a chat. You just follow my lead. I'll call you Brian, though."

"Anything for the woman who invented volunteering."

"I just did the administration."

As they left, Judie grabbed her by the arm earnestly.

"I know this is all illegal but please keep going. Don't let them take away our only time without the kids. We need it."

It had been the local shop owner in Wandsworth who had first told Charlotte that the red car appeared in the evening and left with her to work in the morning. The occupant was always hiding from Charlotte but had not considered that the man in the local shop for whom Charlotte had once obtained some free autographed matchday programmes would have been watching him.

The UK Enforcement Agency received a transcript of the conversation that Charlotte had with Terry before heading back to the football ground that day. It went like this -

Charlotte - "Brian, I can't thank you enough for meeting me here."

Terry - "It's no problem, anything for you, I love your football show."

"You say, all I have to do now is go to the jewellers in the city centre and say that you sent me and they'll show me the stuff that they don't have on display."

"Yes, just say that you've met me and they'll know what to do."

"Look, I've had to sneak out of a football match as cover here, I don't want anyone from the papers getting to know this, you know that they offer a lot of money for stories about me - that's why I had to meet you in that cruddy office block."

"Yeah, how they've not knocked it down, I don't know. You can count on me though, not a word."

"Good, not even Danny knows and can you imagine how much they'd pay for a story about me looking at engagement rings?"

"You can trust me, Charlotte."

"Thanks so much."

Strangely, that was the last report made by the UKEA operative in the Nissan Quinoa. The next day, one of the papers carried an exclusive report that 'Channel 6 Charlotte' had been spotted shopping for an engagement ring and speculating what this could mean for the leggy football-mad lovely. The other papers took up the story the next day, the same day that the operative made his report to UKEA. For some reason, UKEA managers felt that there was something odd about them getting to hear the details of the report after the newspapers and the occupant of the red car soon had a lot of time on his hands to spend his sudden windfall from the previous day's work.

As the information network grew, the government started to make mistakes. A UKEA raid on a mother and toddler group in Pencoed went down very badly as ill-prepared troops tried to deal with screaming toddlers suddenly separated from their mothers.

Employers threatened to sack anyone found volunteering but then quietened down when they realised that some of their most productive and useful workers were the ones secretly involved in the movement and that they could actually improve workers' performance by allowing them time to volunteer.

It was back in London that Charlotte's next initiative started. She was in Danny and Ed's apartment relaxing after a hard week of disguising visits to Volunteer Bureaus with work for the Channel. Things seemed to be going well and they laughed over the outraged newspaper headlines about the Pencoed incident.

"We've got them on the run," said Ed with a smile.

"And Edward here could be the man to take this to the next level," added Danny.

"What do you mean?" asked Charlotte.

"Well," said Ed, "my wine-tasting group has been invited to do something in Parliament next week."

"Great, so six hundred people in the pocket of big business get some free wine?"

Danny looked startled at Charlotte's comment and asked, "Not a voter then?"

"No-one in my family votes," replied Charlotte, "what's the point? We're not the kind of people who politicians care about. No-one is going to leaflet us before 2048 or ask our opinion on anything."

Danny sighed and pondered this, "Sometimes I forget how different your upbringing was to mine. I know where you're coming from, but I have to say that this is a big opportunity for us."

"We're poisoning the wine?"

Ed took over, "When the papers are not covering you and Daniel's never ending on-off romance, they do mention politics. You know that the Opposition has a new leader?"

"I've seen him - youngish guy, keeps talking about energy and initiative and so on."

"I've booked you a meeting with him."

Charlotte shook her head and passed an empty wine glass back to Ed. She stood up and started to pace, "No, I'm no politician. It's one thing being my agent for carpet sales, you can't get me into politics. Anyway, UKEA are following me when they can be bothered, they won't let me in Parliament."

"You'll be smuggled in as a waitress. The Opposition Leader's diary simply states that a waitress from a wine-tasting event will see him for fifteen minutes," replied Ed.

"We've got a new identity for you and everything," added Danny.

"I'm just an administrator, I'm not a political leader though," said Charlotte.

Ed stood up and gave her a big hug, "You're the most organised person, we know. If anyone can work out how to do this, it's you. Here ..."

Ed let go of Charlotte and pulled out something from a drawer beneath the coffee table. It was a blue clear plastic folder and it had a small pink bow attached to it.

"Find out everything you can about him and put the details in here. Then you'll know what to say!"

Charlotte hugged Ed now and said, "You bloody crazy man, you know how to give a good gift! I'd marry you, if I weren't already in a torrid on-off affair with your boyfriend!"

*   *   *   *   *

Charlotte the Sports Reporter turned into Amanda the Waitress for the purposes of the deception. The uniform was pretty standard and - thank goodness for a day on her feet - involved flat shoes. Charlotte pulled her hair up and hoped that with a little less pampering than for the TV studio she would pass unnoticed.

As it was, no-one paid much attention to the waitresses as they entered the Houses of Parliament and the security guards swapped jokes about whether they could impound the wine for searching. She was in.

To be honest, Charlotte disliked Parliament as soon as she saw inside it. The statues in the lobby looked down on her as if they were looking down on her and the oak pannelling and plush-carpeted corridors made her think of what she thought expensive schools were like. Why could Parliament not be like her school or was the point to tell people like her that they did not belong there?

She had memorised every detail that she could find about the Opposition Leader and she formulated a strategy in her head for when the security guards came to collect her for the meeting. Danny and Ed were right, this was an opportunity not to be missed.

Charlotte was armed with her blue plastic folder as she was escorted through the wooden-pannelled corridors of the Palace of Westminster. She fiddled with her uniform tie a little, not used to being reminded of school, but otherwise walked a respectful distance behind them before they were at the office. She was let in.

The Leader of the Opposition looked smaller than he did on television, which started Charlotte wondering if all her fans greeted her with the thought that she was oddly smaller than they had expected. He radiated energy though and jumped up from behind his desk to shake her hand.

"Please call me Greg," he said.

"Amanda," replied Charlotte nervously.

"Is that a Welsh accent?" he asked, before letting go of her hand and indicating for her to sit, "I've been to Wales while campaigning. It's a beautiful country, we're very lucky that you are part of the UK."

Standard flattery thought Charlotte, but he would have prepared for this meeting every bit as much as she had done.

"There is wine grown in South Wales, of course, is that your area?" he asked.

"Yes," replied Charlotte, "our Glyndwr Wine is particularly fine, grown in Llanbethian."

"Excellent, well, you know I want to promote British industry, so it is good to have you here today. What did you want to say?"

Charlotte looked nervously at the security guards and gave Greg a weak smile. It worked.

"Guys - there's no need to hang around, give us some space, you know?" Greg said, thinking that a young Welsh waitress was unlikely to be a threat to anyone.

The security guards left and Charlotte ticked off point three from the mental image she had kept of her to do list. She waited until they had left before she spoke.

"Greg, I have to level with you here. I'm not a waitress, I want to tell you about volunteering and how it can win you the next election."

"You do look familiar from somewhere other than waitressing, but I have to say that I'm confident that we're going to win in 2048."

"Yes, of course and I am sure that the Prime Minister would say that too, but there is no danger in me telling you a few ways to get on the front foot. Your constituency is in Hertfordshire, I believe? Yes? Well, I have had some very interesting dealings with Hertford Volunteer Bureau."

"I've never heard of them."

"Like all the Volunteer Bureaus, they're underground."

"They're in the lower level car park? What do you mean?"

"Some of them are. Let me try to cut to the chase," said Charlotte, fearing that the conversation was already stalling, "I have a list here of people who are volunteering in Hertfordshire, what they do and more importantly, the benefits for them. All the names are anonymous by the way, just in case UKEA are watching you like they're watching me, but these are voters. These are people who you need to put you in power and they love volunteering, either because they do it or because they benefit from it. But your rival has made it illegal as you well know. All of these people could be arrested - you saw what happened to the mothers and toddlers in Pencoed."

Greg studied the piece of paper that Charlotte passed across the desk. He looked as though he was weighing up thoughts carefully. Then again, thought Charlotte, that could be as much an act as any of her roles.

"Aren't all these people taking - no, stealing - British jobs from British workers?"

"Who was losing out from those toddlers meeting and their mothers bonding? No-one. Who is missing out if someone gets together an amateur football team to coach? Who is missing out from support groups for the mentally ill? No-one."

Greg sat back, looked over at Charlotte and shrugged.

"You make a very pervasive case for changing the law, we'll certainly think about suggesting it."

"No, it's not enough. You can't just repeal the law. Volunteering does not come for free. You need training, development, administration, you need a support network. It costs money."

At this point Greg laughed and shook his head, "Amanda, you should know that everyone comes in here asking for money. If only it were that simple ..."

"But it is. The benefits outweigh the expense. You just need to manage it correctly."

"You want me to lead some kind of revolution?" he asked, clicking open a pen and making a few notes.

"No, I'm saying that the revolution has already started. You have a choice to get on board now or be identified with the officers holding the mothers and toddlers apart in Pencoed. It'll happen with you or without you, but if you choose to get involved, that will be your place in history assured."

"My place in history, eh? Perhaps I could get one of my researchers to have a look at it and maybe if the report is favourable ..." started Greg, staring off into the high ceiling of the office thoughtfully.

"No!" said Charlotte, bringing his gaze back down to the table, "You need to commit to funding the infrastructure of the sector and then grants schemes to be delivered by independent voluntary sector bodies in each part of the UK."

"I'm not used to being told what to do, Amanda," he said sharply.

Charlotte wanted to reply that he was the only one in the country who felt like that then, but she restrained herself. Instead, she produced the blue clear plastic folder and handed it to the man opposite her.

Greg grabbed it and stared at the first sheet.

"Basic Waitress Induction?"

"Oh sorry, had to cover it to sneak it in here. The rest is my suggestion for the creation and funding of voluntary sector infrastructure. Page twelve has a breakdown of some comparative costs - for instance, it costs £38,000 per year to keep a young man in a Youth Offenders Institute but you could pay a tenth of that for a voluntary sector youth group to work with him for a year to keep him out of prison. This is right, but it will also save money."

"What's the catch then?" said Greg, putting the folder down and looking across at Charlotte.

"The catch is that all your officials will tell you that it is unworkable. It means giving power to people, ordinary people like me and that will take some guts. Your business backers won't like it, it will spook the money markets but I can tell you now that it will be popular as well as the right thing to do."

"You make it sound appealing, Amanda ..." said Greg.

Yes, thought Charlotte, because I have researched all the major policy decisions that you have approved and written a list of what appeals to you, including your vanity. The only point left is that you like to talk about the need for strong leadership. She smiled the smile of someone who had organised their research well.

"It's all in there, but remember that your advisors will oppose it, you need to be strong to carry this one through."

That would be the list ticked off, then.

Greg stood and shook Charlotte's hand. He looked only partially convinced and Charlotte knew that it partly lay in the hands of focus groups and opinion surveys of potential voters to decide what was right. She had one parting shot as she left the office.

"Have you been to the wine-tasting display?"

"I did pop down there for a cheeky Pinot Grigio, yes. It is a fine job, you should be proud of your Welsh vineyards."

"That's not a trade show today with the wine, that's volunteers running a wine-tasting club."

Charlotte shut the heavy door behind her and waved to the security guards who were loitering in the corridor, unsure of what to do if they were not protecting their boss.

"Don't I know you?" said one of them as Charlotte walked past.

"I don't think so, I'm a waitress with the trade fair. You probably know my sister - Charlotte - she's on TV."

"Oh yeah, you look just like her!"

"Wish I had her money, eh?" she replied and all three of them laughed.

*   *   *   *   *

On the night of the General Election of 2048 – what we now call the Year of Revolutions – Charlotte's Mam had fallen asleep as she had sat on the sofa with her ex-husband. He put a comforting arm around her and looked proudly at the big screen showing footage of their elder daughter. A new government opposed to the anti-volunteering law and committed to establishing a legal footing and dedicated funding for the third sector was sweeping to power. Someone had named Charlotte as an ideal leader for the new funding body or possibly for the new Gender Equality Commission tasked with making discrimination illegal. 'What the Channel 6 sports presenter?' was the question from many, leading to the other breaking news story of the night, how a sports presenter had secretly led a revolution.

The woman herself had been watching on the television in Heather's room and was slowly realising that she needed to speak to her Personal Assistant. She walked across the landing to what was once her own room. Jon was bouncing Jolene up and down on the double bed while Heather typed away on the laptop on her desk.

"Good results coming through, sis," said Heather without looking up.

"Yes, I think that I may have to talk to some people. How's my diary looking for next week?"

Heather opened up a black diary book and frowned at some sticky pages.

"It's looking full of strawberry jam," she said, before turning round and saying across the bed, "Jojo – how many times have I told you not to put jam in your revolutionary auntie's diary?"

"Soon as you can get any of these government people on the phone, let me know. We need a press statement ..."

Charlotte's phone was ringing and she pulled it out of her pocket and answered it.

"Hi Charlotte, it's Ceri. Ceri from Swansea."

"Hi Ceri."

"Do you hear that noise?"

"What you mean the EPICchat noise when you say hello? That's just in your head."

Then in the background Charlotte could hear a crowd of people chanting 'Charlotte! Charlotte!' To her horror, she realised that it was Castle Square in Swansea and that Ceri had named her as the local hero and deliverer of the victory.

"That's mad," said Charlotte, "I'm an administrator."

"No, not now. Now you're Charlotte the Liberator! They'll build statues to you one day!"

"Rubbish," replied Charlotte and tried to remember what she was about to say to her sister about a press statement. Heather was looking very pleased about something.

"It's great," said the younger sister, "we can at least double your appearance fees after this, maybe more."

Charlotte gave her sister a special kind of look of contempt that sisters keep for one other.

"What?" protested Heather, "Gotta pay the bills somehow!"

If you enjoyed this book, why not buy -

The Great Sayings of
Charlotte the Liberator

Edited by Julia Britton

Excerpts from the life and works of the woman
who set the world free.

"The revolution will not be televised,

but it will need an efficient filing system."

Afterword

"Frankly, I am surprised you got this far!" - the end of a letter written by Groucho Marx

Thank you for reading The Tale of Charlotte the Liberator. I hope that you enjoyed it.

If you are interested in more books by Dewi Heald then you can follow me on twitter @dewiheald1 or drop me an e-mail to dewiheald@gmail.com

Why not take a look at my website for all the latest news and regular blogs -

http://dewiheald.wixsite.com/rainbows

You can also buy 'Cheese Market of the Future', a collection of short stories and 'The Seven Pillows of Wisdom', a collection of political essays from Amazon for hard copies or Smashwords for Kindle. Just search on 'Dewi Heald'-I am the one and only!

Interview

with the Author

This novella was first launched at the Llanbethian Literary Festival and here is a short transcript of an interview given by the author to interviewer Kerry Preston at a festival event –

KP : Dewi Heald, today is the launch of The Tale of Charlotte the Liberator, where did the idea for it come from?

DH : Thanks Kerry, I am pleased to be here. Charlotte's tale started as a dream I had one Saturday night. I dreamt that I was visiting Orchard House in Swansea and there was a voluntary sector group there – I'm not sure which charity – but they were having trouble taking up the carpet and they kept saying 'we need Charlotte the Administrator'. It made me think about how people undervalue administrators. They hold everything together – especially in the voluntary sector – and yet they're always the first people whose jobs are cut. I thought it would be interesting to write a story where the hero is the administrator. So, the next morning on a bus to Cardiff I wrote a short story about Charlotte.

KP : It was a short story, then?

DH : Oh yes, the short story 'Charlotte the Administrator' is in a collection somewhere. I forgot to add that before catching the bus I watched the football highlights, I think that you can see that in the story as well.

KP : This is a novella though rather than a short story. How did this version come about?

DH : That was because the New Welsh Review launched their novella competition the next week and I thought that it would make a good novella.

KP : Are there sections which you would want to extend, perhaps make it a full length book?

DH : I have thought about that. I'm tempted to write more about the revolutionary movement and how it takes hold and so on – we also move through Charlotte's time in administration fairly quickly, but for all it skips over a lot of details, I quite like the fast pace of only having 30,000 words to tell the story in. I don't think that it needs to be extended.

KP : It's set in the future. Do you think that this will mean it is pigeon-holed as a fantasy or sci-fi book?

DH : I hope not. It's not really the future though, that's just a convenient way of saying that it's a different world. A world where people only value things for money, where everything is seen as a financial transaction? We're on the way to that. A society where women's rights are going backwards, where if you want to be rich you have to be born rich? I'd ask the reader how far we are from that, really. It's the future, but it's really a reflection on how we are living today.

KP : What would you like people to take away from this book?

DH : I'd like the reader to think 'I must buy more books by this author – lots of copies to give to all my friends as well'. No, seriously, I don't mind if people enjoy the jokes or if they want to take a bigger message away from it. I do think that there is something to be said about the voluntary sector, charities to most people, and how they hold things together but they are subject to huge attacks by government and the media. And I would like people to take away something about administrators of course, everyone be nice to administrators.

KP : Would you like to write more about Charlotte the Liberator in future?

DH : I think that 'Charlotte : The Early Years' has been done already in the first chapter somehow!

KP : How important is it for you to write about local places?

DH : I do think that there are too many books about New York or Los Angeles or even Prague or Rome and not enough about the people who live outside big cities ...

KP : Are you worried that people from London will be insulted by it?

DH : I like London, I just wanted to give an idea of the politics and media of the UK being completely concentrated on the city. Charlotte's world is one of low expectation – she knows from birth what is expected of her and that is very little. Lots of people live with that and with the idea that if something exciting is happening then it is happening elsewhere. It almost does not matter whether she has any talent or not. That's true of some of the Londoners she meets though.

KP : Do you think that that is true though? Could she have stayed in Barry and had a successful career?

DH : That's her society though, there is no or very little mobility. I also like Barry – I used to walk from the station to a job in the northern suburbs so I was walking up impossibly steep hills and I saw Aberystwyth Crescent one day and I know the life of living in a terraced house and it seemed to fit. It could be any number of towns really. But I like Barry and I was happy to write about it.

Thinking about your other question, I might do The Further Adventures of Heather the Younger Sister! I think that she might be quite interesting. Though no-one notices how Charlotte starts out calling her 'the sister' and she only becomes 'my sister' when they start to co-operate.

Also, no-one notices that no-one has a surname!

KP : Was that deliberate?

DH : Not really. In the short story, Ladislau appears as Ladislau Heron I think. I realised though that Charlotte's family did not have a surname and I thought that it might be interesting to write the whole thing without any surnames used – perhaps it echoes the way people are owned by their jobs and lose their identity to them … I'm not sure … it just amused me that no-one has pointed that out yet.

KP : Except the police officers.

DH : I thought that it would be fun if they had no first names, just as a contrast!

KP : Thank you Dewi for your time here today.

DH : *Diolch yn fawr*, my pleasure.

19329868R00085

Printed in Poland
by Amazon Fulfillment
Poland Sp. z o.o., Wrocław